RAISING STEAM

RAISING STEAM

The design, operation and driving of steam locomotives

DENIS GRIFFITHS
C.Eng, B.Eng, M.Sc, F.I.Mar.E.

PSL

Patrick Stephens Limited

British Library Cataloguing in Publication Data
Griffiths, Denis, *1943–*
    Raising steam.
    1. Steam locomotives, to 1980
    I. Title
    625.2'61'09

    ISBN 1-85260-077-2

Patrick Stephens Limited is part of the Thorsons Publishing Group, Wellingborough, Northamptonshire, NN8 2RQ, England.

Typeset by Burns & Smith, Derby

Printed and bound in Great Britain by Butler & Tanner Ltd, Frome and London

10   9   8   7   6   5   4   3   2

Contents

Dedication

For
Geoff Johnson
my friend
and fellow enthusiast

Introduction

One of the most remarkable attributes of the steam locomotive is that it will continue to work when in a generally run-down condition where the diesel locomotive, for example, will fail if some of its equipment only marginally deteriorates. In comparison with the diesel or electric locomotive the steam locomotive is basic 'low tech'. Historically this has been one of its most useful advantages, allowing for maintenance and repair in fairly crude environments and with unsophisticated tools. By contrast, steam locomotive operation requires a degree of skill because the operator is in sole charge and this also contrasts with the diesel or electric where control systems will ensure that the 'engine' part of the plant only works within planned limits. This is not to denigrate in any way the high degree of driving skill required from the man in the cab of a diesel or electric locomotive, but to emphasize the steam crew's direct control over their machine.

The 'low technology' steam locomotive changed little in basic form from the days of Stephenson until the demise of steam traction on British Railways in that it still consisted of a boiler and an engine unit to drive the wheels. The actual machines which saw out steam in Britain were much more complex than their earlier brothers, but they would still tolerate the rundown condition — in fact they had to. Efficiency suffered if the engine or boiler sections deteriorated but deterioration in performance of the braking system could not be tolerated: even the most basic of machines have critical parts.

Brakes are an obvious essential but injector failure preventing water from being fed to the boiler meant that the locomotive had to be stopped. Bearings and other items were tolerant of condition but there were limits which, when reached, resulted in failure. Fuel economy and performance were important and efficient draughting arrangements became an essential feature for economic performance of draughting. Several systems were developed, some better than others for certain purposes, but they all relied upon a draught produced by exhausting steam. Although simple in concept these different draughting systems were very complex affairs relying on involved mathematics for design and they could deteriorate dramatically when operated away from design limits but they would still work! At the end of the British steam era the steam locomotive did rely upon some high level technology but the design remained such that operation was still possible when conditions were less than perfect.

This book aims to describe the operation of the steam locomotive, looking at each part of its machinery in turn. I have avoided any thought of detailed mathematics which was an essential in any original good design: the language will be straightforward and non-technical. I have not followed a particular company or even a class of locomotive, instead it is the systems which are described, using examples found on certain locomotives. Where fundamentally different arrangements have been used to serve the same purpose they will, generally, be described, e.g. vacuum pumps and air ejectors for brake systems. In general I have used the present tense because many steam locomotives are preserved and it is to the operation of these that the book is directed. This is not a history book but one that aims to help towards an understanding of the steam locomotive as it still exists. Steam locomotives disappeared from Britain's main lines over twenty years ago but preserved locomotives work in exactly the same way as they did in those far-off days, the only real difference being that they are generally much better cared for than those in the 1960s. Sight of a preserved locomotive in action will back-up the information in this book and it is a tribute to many hundreds of steam enthusiasts that preserved locomotives are here now to be enjoyed and appreciated in their reality.

Engineeering principles are not difficult to understand and appreciate but the railway enthusiast with his interest in locomotives, rolling stock and equipment, need not become involved in the engineering mathematics at too deep a level in order to understand the operation. In addition to explaining how each part of the steam locomotive works I also hope to provide some understanding as to *why* it works. This is not a technical manual on locomotive design but is intended as an aid to knowledge, and knowledge is, or should be, a pleasure. It is within the grasp of every railway enthusiast to understand the workings of the steam locomotive and then he will appreciate not only the sight of the machine at work but also the beauty of the engineering.

CHAPTER 1

The locomotive

The dictionary definition of a locomotive is an engine which moves by its own power. The steam locomotive achieves movement by the use of steam and thus there are two fundamental parts of a steam locomotive namely the device for producing steam, a boiler, and the mechanism for making use of it, the engine. Each is effectively a separate item but the machine can only function if both are working. The engine part relies entirely upon the boiler for its working fluid, steam, but the boiler also depends upon the engine to some extent in that exhaust steam from the engine is used to create a draught in order that better fuel combustion can take place. With many early locomotives water could only be supplied to the boiler by means of a pump operated by the engine unit, but that dependence disappeared with the invention of the injector.

An engine unit may consist of two, three or four cylinders (more with Garratt, Mallet and other special locomotives) and these require valve gear in order to ensure that steam supply and exhaust is correct both in timing and quantity. Valve gear can be simplified to the extent that a single set may operate valves for two cylinders, but its accurate setting is critical to efficient performance. Reciprocating parts set up forces which need to be balanced but the use of balancing weights produces other forces which may aggravate the situation.

Other auxiliary systems also apply to the locomotive directly or to the train it is intended to pull. Brakes are an obvious requirement but passenger trains also need heating in cold weather and that can come from steam supplied by the boiler unit. Apart from special condensing types the locomotive discharges steam when it has passed through the cylinders and so a reserve water supply must be carried in

An example of a tender locomotive: Bulleid 'West Country' 'Pacific' No 34029, City of Wells.

Tank locomotive of 2-6-2 form: Churchward design '45xx' Class No 4555.

tanks or tender. Long non-stop runs would require large tenders or an ability to collect a fresh supply whilst in motion. The water trough and pick-up apparatus became standard for many tender locomotives as well as a number of tank types.

Although the steam locomotive can be considered rather primitive compared with a diesel locomotive, it is nevertheless a fairly complex affair made up of many interrelated parts all performing set functions. Good design and development kept the steam locomotive at work on the world's railways for over 150 years and few other concepts can be said to have lasted so well.

The structure of the locomotive

Before considering the boiler and engine units in detail it is necessary to look at the overall locomotive structure. For our purposes for the moment the only difference between tender and tank locomotives lies in the fact that the latter carry their coal and water supply on the main structure rather than behind in a separate unit.

The main frames form the locomotive's foundation and carry the boiler and cylinders along with all other items necessary for the machine to function. Provision must be made on the frame for axleboxes and spring gear. Axleboxes provide bearings which allow for wheel rotation and they must be supplied with oil in order that wear of the bearing material (usually some form of tin-based white metal) does not become excessive. For most modern locomotives a mechanical lubricator would be used to deliver oil to the top of each axlebox, thus ensuring an oil film at all times. Loss of lubrication, the presence of dirt or overload of the bearing due to heavy running, could result in bearing failure, something for which the footplate crew had to be vigilant in regular service and still something to watch for with preserved steam operations.

The use of roller bearings avoids many of the problems associated with bearings of white metal but effective lubrication is still essential. Lubricated by oil or grease, roller-bearing axleboxes require considerably less attention than the plain bearing type.

Although their prime purpose is to allow the wheels to rotate, axleboxes also have to slide in hornblocks in order to allow for springing. Correct alignment of the hornblocks is essential as any slight misalignment will result in excessive forces on the bearings due to the loads imparted by the pistons. Hornblocks are bolted or riveted either side of slots in the frame or, in the case of horseshoe pattern hornblocks, riveted all round. Excessive wear at the hornblocks is compensated for by the periodic renewal of the brass rubbing strips fitted on the axlebox side faces. Slight misalignment can be corrected by off-centre boring of the axleboxes. It is essential that axles are aligned relative to each other and that cylinders are correctly aligned with the axles with which they are to connect. Any error in positioning imparts excessive loads on coupling and connecting rod bushes, increasing wear. Collett, during his time as Chief Mechanical Engineer (CME) on the GWR, instituted a system of optical alignment which improved considerably the time between the shopping of locomotives for bearing correction.

Spring gear fitted at each axlebox serves to transmit loads to the axles, controls the rise of axleboxes in the hornblocks and dampens out track shocks. Laminated leaf springs positioned below the axles were usually found to provide the best arrangement for British locomotives. For overseas railways with poor track some form of compensation was generally employed, groups of axles being connected to sets of springs by compensating levers, thus distributing track imperfections over a number of axles.

British practice employed plate frames but overseas bar frames were more common, again because of lower standard track. The basic difference lies in the fact that bar frames are

Locomotive frames and structure.

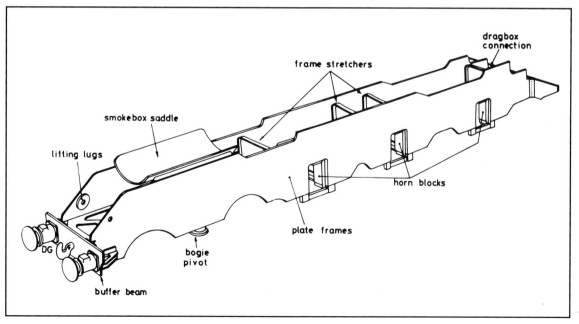

shallower and of thicker section than plate frames, the increased thickness allowing hornblocks to be dispensed with. Plate frames, about 1.25 in (16mm) thick, consist of two mild steel plates cut to shape and connected by means of stretchers to give rigidity and correct positioning. A smokebox saddle, buffer beam and dragbox are also incorporated although the smokebox saddle might be part of the cylinder casting. Pivot pins for bogie and trailing wheel sets as well as brake hanger brackets would be fitted as necessary.

Welding provided the more usual post-war method of frame construction but earlier frames were riveted. The dragbox and its drawbar linkage connects engine unit to tender and must be substantial enough to transmit the entire pull exerted on tender and train and provide flexibility at the same time. The drawbar itself is often spring-loaded but alternative-ly a solid drawbar can be used with spring-loaded buffers on the tender to keep the drawbar in tension and allow for flexibility. Buffer beams require similar substantial connection to the frames.

The basic purpose of a bogie or pony truck is to lead and guide a locomotive into and out of curves, thus ensuring safety at high speed. Some degree of support is also provided at the front end, this being particularly important on locomotives with cylinders placed well forward. The function of a trailing wheelset (whether bogie or pony truck) under a wide firebox is to carry the weight of that firebox where its width does not allow the fitting of an additional coupled axle.

Driving wheels and axles differ in construction and number depending upon the type of locomotive and the arrangement of the cylinders. Axles are straight or cranked depending

Right *Inside the cranked driving axle of a GWR locomotive, showing the bottom end bearing and valve eccentric connections.*

Below left *Drawbar connections at the rear of a Riddles 'Austerity' 2–10–0 type locomotive.*

upon whether the locomotive has inside cylinders or not (inside cylinders requiring cranks). High quality steel has to be employed for this critical component, sections being machined in order to provide journals for the axlebox bearings. For larger locomotives cranked axles are of built-up construction which means that shaft sections, crank webs and pins are all separate parts connected together by means of force fits and keys. Where outside cylinders are used cranks may be cast as part of the wheel centres, allowing for straight axles which minimize constructional difficulties. In many cases axles are hollow to save weight without reducing strength.

Spoked wheels applied to the majority of British locomotives but adherence to the spoked pattern was probably more the result of tradition than for any other reason. A locomotive wheel actually consists of two parts: a wheel centre, comprising hub, spokes and rim, and a steel tyre shrunk on the outer face of the rim. Cast from high quality steel, wheel centres for driving wheels with outside cylinders are also provided with a cast-in crank, subsequently machined out to take the force-fitted crank pin. Bulleid locomotives on the Southern railway employed box pattern wheel centres which were not only attractive but stronger and lighter than spoked wheels of the same size. These Bulleid-Firth-Brown wheels also avoided the problem of fractured spokes and the tendency of spoked wheel centres to distort. Riddles 'Austerity' 2–8–0 and 2–10–0 locomotives have solid wheels of 'I' section fitted on pony trucks, but use spoked driving wheels.

Wheels are a forced fit onto axles with a key, or keys, providing the final connection. When assembling a wheeled axle, or any cranked axle, care has to be taken to ensure that cranks are correctly positioned relative to each other. Keyways already machined in axles, hubs and cranks assist in such positioning provided that they have been cut correctly.

It is not the wheel rims which run on the rails but separately fitted steel tyres. After a period of wear these tyres can be reprofiled by machining but when an upper limit of tread wear is reached they require replacement to avoid the danger of bursting due to the centrifugal stress imposed by the wheel's rotation whilst the locomotive runs at high speed. Al-

Above *'Austerity' 2–10–0 locomotive No 90775 on the Mid-Hants Railway. The solid pony truck wheels may be seen.*

Below *Tyre fitting arrangements.*

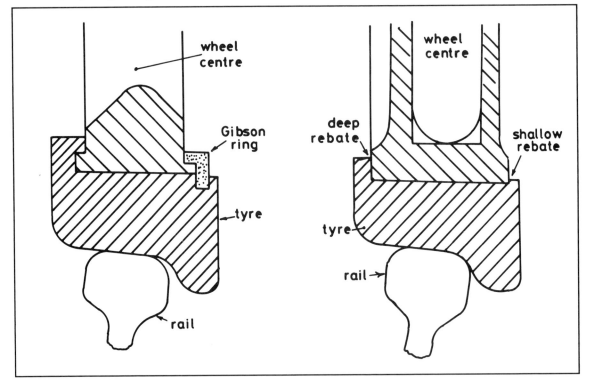

though the tyre is sometimes riveted to the wheel the shrinkage fit is the only suitable method for strength. In order to provide sufficient force between tyre and rim the tyre must be smaller than the rim, a shrinkage allowance of about 1 in 1,000 usually being sufficient, e.g. for every metre of rim diameter the tyre is 1 mm smaller. To shrink-fit the tyre onto the wheel the tyre is heated, thus expanding the metal sufficiently for it to fit on the wheel rim.

Tyres can still work sideways off the rim and some locking system is usually considered desirable. The Gibson ring method found favour with the GWR and LMS whilst a rebate arrangement was employed by Bulleid and for BR standard classes (see the drawing opposite). After fitting, tyres are profiled to suit the track profile. Although flanges are provided on most tyres the flanges are not intended to rub against the rail in normal running. Correct tyre and rail profiles keep wheels, and hence the locomotive, correctly positioned on the rails. The opposing slopes of tyres and rails basically force the locomotive towards a central position between the rails. Flanges provide a safeguard to staying on the rails especially on bends but they can be a hindrance on tight curves or where more than three coupled axles are provided. Some locomotives were prohibited from using tightly curved track, especially at speed, because, amongst other reasons, tightly curved rails impose considerable side forces on wheel flanges. To minimize this particular problem certain classes, notably the 'Austerity' 2–10–0s and 2–10–0 BR standard '9Fs', have flangeless wheels on the centre driving axle and flanges of reduced thickness on wheels fitted to the second and fourth driving axles.

CHAPTER 2

The boiler

A steam locomotive's working fluid is, naturally, steam — which has to be generated from water, hence the fitting of a boiler. Before considering boiler construction and operation it is worth looking at the basic process of steam generation. For practical reasons concerning power requirements and engineering components steam used in the cylinders cannot be returned to the boiler in order to receive further heat and have its pressure increased. Pumping steam into the boiler against boiler pressure would require as much energy as the steam gave up in the cylinders, hence no useful work would be achieved. It is much simpler and a more effective process, to pump a liquid (water) into the boiler and convert that into steam for use in the engine. At this point it is worth mentioning that the reheating of 'partly used' steam is possible in order to increase its temperature, but not its pressure. Such reheating was frequently employed with marine steam turbine engines in order to avoid condensation in the turbine but the idea was not feasible for steam locomotives where single stage expansion is used, nor for that matter with compound locomotives.

Water in a boiler first receives heat which produces a rise in temperature. This, in effect, is a waste as the boiler is at its most efficient employed only for steam generation. Heat can be applied in external feed heaters or in the injector but if the water temperature is too high injectors or pumps will not function correctly.

One way around the problem is to heat the water after the pump or injector and such an arrangement was employed with the Crosti boiler in which flue gases heated the feed. An idea of the amount of sensible heat which must be supplied in order to raise water to boiling temperature can be gauged from the time it takes for a kettle to boil. The amount of gas burned or electricity consumed is appreciable and the energy involved in just heating water is wasted as far as the locomotive is concerned.

At a particular temperature, the saturation temperature, further addition of heat will convert water into steam. This is the latent heat of evaporation and as the water evaporates there is no further increase in temperature. Each pressure has its own evaporation or saturation temperature: the higher the pressure the higher will be the evaporation temperature. At normal atmospheric pressure of one bar or 100 kN/m^2 (14.5 psi) water boils at 100°C (212°F) but at 17.24 bar or $1,724 \text{ kN/m}^2$ (250 psi) the boiling temperature will be 205°C (401°F).

A considerable amount of heat has to be expended simply converting water into steam in addition to that heat required to raise feed water temperature to the evaporation temperature. Some heat is recovered in the cylinders because of the expansive properties of steam but the 'sensible' heat can never be recovered and represents a complete loss. The higher the pressure the greater the potential for expansion but high pressures cause boiler design problems

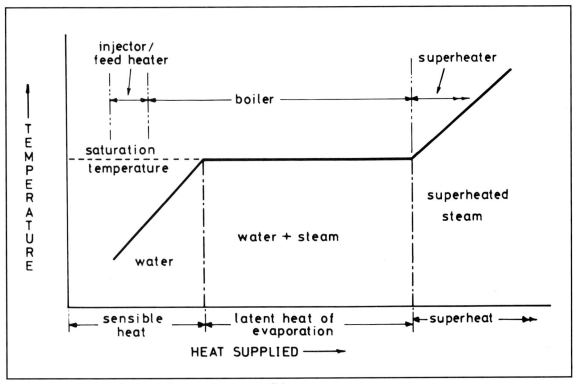

Graph showing heat input and water/steam conditions.

and increase the amount of sensible heat required.

When all of the latent heat has been supplied steam is said to be dry and saturated, it contains no water droplets. That condition will exist so long as there is some water present in the boiler shell as no further increase in temperature can take place if water is anywhere in contact with the steam. By removing steam from the steam generating region its temperature may be increased by the addition of more heat, super-heating, this usually being accomplished by passing the steam through tubes located within large flue tubes. Use of superheated steam has other advantages which will be discussed later but drying out steam in this manner gives less risk of condensation occurring in the cylinders and hence the maximum expansive working of the steam can be obtained.

This then describes the basic steam generating cycle of any boiler. In that most heat cannot be recovered in the cylinders, it should be fairly clear that the use of steam is inefficient. Heat is provided in order to produce a working fluid, steam, from the non-working fluid, water, and only the energy contained within the steam by virtue of its pressure can possibly be recovered in the cylinders. The steam which produces highly photogenic exhaust patterns is a complete waste of energy!

Construction

In terms of construction a locomotive boiler is a single unit containing two sections, water side and gas side, which may be treated separately for descriptive purposes. Although water-tube boilers have been tried from time to time the type of boiler applicable to the steam locomotive in general is the fire tube type of the form fitted in Stephenson's *Rocket*. Over the years detail changes have taken place but the basic

Long Belpaire boiler of the preserved LMS 'Pacific' No 6201, Princess Elizabeth.

structure remains, a barrel containing tubes which connect firebox and chimney and through which pass the products of fuel combustion. Water surrounds the tubes and firebox with a steam space being provided at the upper portion.

Boiler size and arrangement obviously depend upon the size of locomotive but the subject can be discussed in general terms with reference being made to specific cases where necessary. Although welding of pressure vessels was possible towards the end of steam locomotive construction for British Railways, riveting remained the usual form of manufacture. A boiler barrel would be made from mild steel plates 13 mm to 19 mm (0.5 in to 0.75 in) thick depending upon operating pressure. These plates, between one and two metres wide, would be rolled into circular rings of the correct diameter and double riveted using cover plates inside and out. A number of such rings

made up a complete barrel which might, in some cases, be tapered towards the front. A tubeplate, about 25 mm thick and usually of mild steel, though sometimes of copper, closed the barrel at the front end.

The firebox end of the boiler consists of two parts comprising inner and outer fireboxes. The outer firebox is basically an extension of the boiler barrel, being made from mild steel plate of similar thickness. Sometimes known as 'the wrapper' the outer firebox is shaped to a particular design which must suit the inner firebox and provide sufficient steam space. A single plate is bent to form the top and sides which are then hot riveted to the mild steel foundation ring. A single plate is also used to form the rear end of the firebox, this being deeply flanged at top and sides in order to allow riveting to the wrapper plate. A connection is made with the foundation ring at the bottom. A front end plate of similar flanged form completes the outer firebox and allows connection with the barrel.

In British practice the inner firebox is usually made from good quality copper but steel has been used by some designers. Copper was used because of its higher heat conductivity and greater ductility which allowed variations in thermal stress caused by changes in firing rate to be more easily countered. Construction is similar to that for the outer firebox with flanged plates being riveted to each other and to the foundation ring. The order in which parts were assembled depended upon design but ease of construction had priority.

High boiler pressure pushes on the inner firebox whilst an outward force is exerted on the outer firebox. Curved surfaces, cylindrical or spherical, can resist higher pressures more easily than flat surfaces for the same plate thickness. (This is why pressurized aerosol containers have concave and convex ends.) To support a given pressure, the plate thickness for a flat surface would need to be much greater than that for a curved surface and thicker plates increase weight and cost as well as reducing heat transfer. The use of stays between surfaces subject to opposing forces also allows for a considerable reduction in plate thickness with all of the benefits that produces. Locomotive fireboxes, however, invariably have extensive flat surfaces making stays necessary for strengthening. Connecting the outer firebox, which is being forced outwards by steam pressure, to the inner firebox which is tending to collapse, allows each to lend support to the other. Stays may be of copper, steel or monel metal and the pattern differs with location. Within the water spaces at the sides and ends of inner and outer fireboxes a fairly simple arrangement of screwed stays is employed. Copper stays are usually riveted over after screwing into position but steel stays are provided with nuts which must just reach the end of the threaded portion. Water space stays are pitched about 100 mm (4 in) apart.

Firebox crown or roof stays were originally of the girder type which passed immediately over the inner firebox top acting like reinforcement beams. The disadvantage of this design is that the beams tended to interfere with water circulation and the rise of steam bubbles. The stays also made washing out and descaling difficult. Direct staying minimized these problems and became more common practice. Similar in form to water space stays the screwed-direct stays may be held by nuts at each end or only at the inner firebox end with riveting providing a seal at the outer firebox. Such direct stays provide good support but they do not allow for upward thermal expansion of the inner firebox. Effects of this expansion, and contraction, are most severe towards the front of the inner firebox, known as the breaking zone, and a form of flexible, or indirect,

Sectional diagram of a typical boiler.

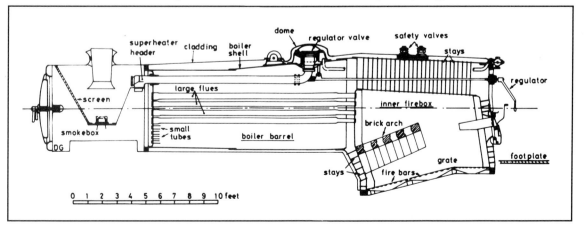

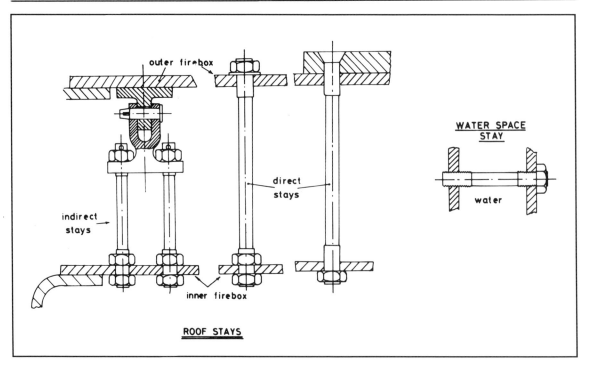

outer firebox

WATER SPACE
STAY

water

direct
stays

indirect
stays

inner firebox

ROOF STAYS

Above *Firebox roof and side stays.*

Left *Lower corner section of boiler outer firebox, showing stays, washout plug holes and cleaning holes.*

Right *Flue tubes with welded ends having screw threads.*

staying is used to allow for relative movement.

Transverse stays tie the outer firebox sides between rows of roof stays above the inner firebox. Belpaire fireboxes with their relatively flat sides allow for easy screw thread and nut connections. A round top firebox has its transverse stays screwed into the plates then riveted or bolted to angle irons riveted to the circular roof plates.

Gusset stays made from angle plate connect the front tubeplate with the boiler barrel but tube plates do not require a major system of stays because of the staying effect provided by the tubes. In the steam space, however, where there are no tubes, a number of long stays connect front tube plate with the back of the outer firebox.

Tubes, generally of steel, vary in size, number and disposition depending upon the boiler but where superheaters are fitted large flues as well as smaller diameter tubes must be provided in order to accommodate superheater elements. Large flues might be about 125 mm (5 in) diameter and small tubes about 50 mm (2 in) diameter. It is usual to have separate ends welded or brazed onto tube lengths. This simplifies manufacture and allows expensive flues to be reused after removal, provided that they are still satisfactory, only the ends having to be renewed.

Tubes are expanded into their tubeplate holes using a special tool, the expanded connection being leak-proof although re-expanding might become necessary after a period in service. In many cases ferrules are driven into the tubes, especially at the firebox end, in order to protect the expanded connection. Common practice has flue tubes screwed into the firebox tubeplate, the ends then being beaded over in order to form a seal. Later practice saw the use of seal welding at tube ends. For reasons which are obvious from the sectional drawing of a boiler (see page 19) tubes are inserted, and removed, through the smokebox tubeplate. To

allow for this holes in that tubeplate must be larger than the nominal outside tube diameter, hence tube ends for the smokebox tubeplate must be larger than the tube outside diameter.

Fire side

Below the inner firebox is the grate upon which coal is burnt. Cast iron firebars should provide an air space of not less than 33 per cent of the grate area and generally up to 50 per cent in order to allow passage of air for good combustion. Damper area should be about 20 per cent of the grate area. Firebars are placed lengthwise in the grate, their ends being supported by a frame. Bar spacing is such that there is good air flow through but ash can fall from the fire base into the ashpan. Some locomotives were fitted with dropping grates in which front sections of the grate could be lowered by means of a pivot and lever arrangement so as to assist in fire removal. In other cases rocking grates were employed. As the name implies the bars could be given a rocking motion by means of a system of levers located in the cab thus breaking up clinker and allowing ash to fall more easily through the bars. The same levers could be used to pivot the bars at something approaching right angles to discharge the entire grate contents into the ashpan for disposal.

Early locomotives had horizontal grates but most large main-line locomotives of the 20th century were fitted with sloping grates. Such a design was useful with large grates for it eased the fireman's job in that coal would gradually work its way to the front of the box. Size of grate had to suit the total evaporative surface area of the boiler and for British locomotives grate area varied between 1/50th and 1/60th of the total evaporation area. A small grate area with a vigorous fire would generate heat but the large draught necessary for such combustion could draw unburnt coal particles through tubes thereby reducing efficiency. Theoretically fireboxes can be any size but the area for hand firing is limited by the abilities of the fireman. An LMS Duchess's 4.65 sq metre (50

sq ft) represents the largest used in normal British practice but its boiler was never pushed to the limit.

Large grates, and hence higher evaporation rates, are possible but to work more efficiently require some form of mechanical stoker. These were never popular in Britain although the American-designed Berkley stoker was fitted to three standard Class '9Fs', with their 3.72 sq metre (40 sq ft) grates, during 1958. Because of that relatively small grate area results were no better than for hand firing but the difference was that the mechanically stoked '9Fs' could maintain maximum steaming rate continuously. In practice this was no advantage since traffic could not be found for exploitation of continuous full power. British builders did, however, construct locomotives for overseas railways with such devices. The North British-built Class '25' locomotives for South African Railways have 6.51 sq metre (70 sq ft) grates fed by screw stokers which discharge coal onto a delivery plate inside the firehole, controllable steam jets then directing it to particular parts of the grate. Only with such large grates and a requirement for sustained maximum evaporation rate were mechanical stokers ever really justified.

In order to avoid long grates, which made firing difficult, the wide firebox was used but that also presented problems in that driving wheels got in the way. Solutions were to employ pony trucks or bogies below the firebox or pitch the boiler high enough to allow the firebox to clear the wheels. Limited loading gauge in Britain frequently restricted the latter option. The Garratt design, however, provided a further alternative: in this case the boiler can be any size or shape, within the load gauge limits, because it does not actually sit above the driving wheels.

A major factor in boiler design is the firebox volume. It must be large enough to allow for complete combustion of volatile matter in the fuel before the gases enter the tubes. Optimum size for a particular grate area depends upon the type of fuel being burnt and as coal quality varies no ideal could ever be produced to suit all conditions. Some 40–45 per cent of heat liberated by combustion passes to the water through the firebox plates, the remainder is transferred via the tubes. An increased volume firebox, at the expense of some tube length, can be obtained by a forward extension above the brick arch thus forming a combustion chamber immediately before the tubes.

An important feature of any firebox is the brick arch. Erected above the grate and immediately below the first row of tubes, the arch slopes upwards towards the firehole door and its purpose is to direct volatile matter liberated from the coal in that direction. This allows combustible gases to mix with air entering above the fire and ensures complete combustion without smoke. A deflector or baffle fitted in the firebox just above the door directs this secondary air downwards into the flame and gas path. Arch and baffle are designed to act in combination, if one does not suit the other then incorrect mixing, and hence inefficient combustion, takes place. After a period of prolonged service baffle and/or arch can become damaged resulting in a fall-off in performance. The fireman's skill in maintaining a good fire with correct air flow below and above will minimize smoke and ensure maximum efficiency.

Water and steam side

Water in the boiler not only forms steam but in doing so it keeps the metal parts cooler than they would otherwise be. Overheating, especially of the firebox, can be disastrous as it weakens the metal resulting in catastrophic failure. If the boiler water level falls below the top of the firebox crown, collapse may take place and high pressure water can be forced into the furnace and hence the cab. The footplate crew would stand little chance of survival. Low water level can be the result of a false gauge glass reading, the failure of the injectors or even an empty tank but vigilance should avoid the problem. However, if the level

does fall fusible plugs provide a safeguard against collapse. These devices, made of copper or steel and containing a lead plug, screw into the firebox crown. Any water covering the crown keeps them relatively cool but if they are uncovered, even momentarily, the lead will melt allowing steam into the firebox and giving an audible and visual warning that the fire must be dropped or extinguished immediately in order to prevent further damage. The melting or 'dropping' of a plug is looked upon with a degree of scorn because it is usually the symptom of neglect.

Any water obtained from usual sources contains levels of dissolved salts which will cause priming, or remain in the boiler once the water has been evaporated. Distilled water as used for marine and power station boilers is not a practical proposition for locomotives. It is not necessary to give details of these scale-forming salts or even to consider the chemical reactions which take place within the boiler so long as the reader understands that chemical problems do result from the heating and evaporation of water. A number of lineside water softening plants were installed in Britain but no general system could be adopted because of the difference in water quality between various regions, and even within regions. The same problems prevented 'on board' treatment systems, such as the French TIA (*Traitement Integral Armand*) adopted by Bulleid on the Southern Railway, being more widely used.

Despite the problems it was accepted that the use of treated water increased the interval between boiler washouts. The problem of scale formation can be appreciated by again considering the domestic kettle. After a number of days in use scale may be observed to form on metal parts (the plastic surface of most modern electric kettles does not provide a good key for the scale but nobody would consider a high pressure and temperature *plastic* boiler ideal). This scale is only that which precipitates following heating of the water, complete evaporation does not (or should not!) take place in a domestic kettle. If water was completely evaporated, as it is in a boiler, considerably more scale would form. Scale forms an insulating layer on metal surfaces and so reduces heat transfer. This not only reduces efficiency but can be dangerous as the subsequent overheating can weaken parts of the boiler.

Treatment, as already mentioned, can reduce the problem but never eliminate it. The great designer Churchward adopted a novel approach on the GWR. His top feed arrangement introduced feed water at the top of a boiler onto a tray within the steam space. This feed was heated on the tray rather than in the water space, a method that resulted in deposition of much of the scale-forming impurities on the tray: trays could be removed periodically for cleaning.

Treatment of water with chemicals can increase the risk of priming. This is basically the carry-over of water droplets with the steam due to aggressive boiling of the water. This can cause problems in the cylinders and other steam-operated parts of the locomotive. Showers of water from the chimney indicate the problem whilst whistles sound rather odd when operated on a mixture of steam and water rather than pure steam. White deposits on boiler cladding around whistles, safety valves and even chimneys are a good indication that priming has taken place.

Blowing down whilst under steam can reduce salt concentration within the water space and thus restrict the likelihood of priming and minimize scale formation on heating surfaces. The LMS operated a system of continuous blowdown on some of its locomotives, a small quantity of water being continuously blown out of the boiler when the regulator was open. A blowdown valve, controlled by steam from the steam chest, allowed water to be discharged from the boiler onto the track ballast through a cooling coil in the tender or side water tanks. The cooling coil ensured that only water was discharged with little visible sign that any blowdown was taking place. In other parts of the world a more spectacular form of blowdown takes place. Direct blowdown produces masses of steam in a long jet as hot high-pressure water is rapidly reduced to atmospheric pressure. South African steam locomotives use relatively poor quality water and regular blowdown is essential. At depots blowdown towers are provided which direct the plumes of steam upwards but on the road jets blast outwards from the locomotive sides for many metres. In the vast wastes of the Karoo there is no likelihood of injuring anyone but such an arrangement would never have been allowed on a British railway.

Even with water treatment and blowdown boilers eventually do need to be descaled, an operation performed at a washout. Boilers are provided with washout plugs and inspection doors at various locations, these must be removed carefully and numbered so that they are replaced in the same location. A high-pressure water jet is directed through these openings into the scaled-up surfaces, the jet nozzles being small enough to pass between the stays. At the same time rods are used to rake accessible scale free. The interval between washouts depends upon the quality of the water used in the boiler, any treatment or blowdown and the daily operating hours.

For most main-line British locomotives the flat-topped inner firebox became standard practice because its shape allowed for a less cluttered form of staying which in turn made for easier release of steam bubbles and descaling. Round-topped inner fireboxes became the preserve of small shunting and industrial locomotives. The Belpaire firebox with its flat topped outer casing also became popular with many designers although there was never any real evidence that it was stronger or allowed for better steaming than the round-topped variety. Personal preference played an important part in design but whichever form was chosen it was essential that ample steam space was provided between inner and outer fireboxes. The Belpaire type certainly provided that.

Effective water circulation around the inner firebox is also essential in order to provide effective steam generation and avoid stagnant

Above *Belpaire form of boiler as fitted to Maunsell 'N' Class 2-6-0 No 31874.*

Below *Round top form of boiler as fitted to Maunsell 'N15' Class 4-6-0 No 777,* Sir Lamiel.

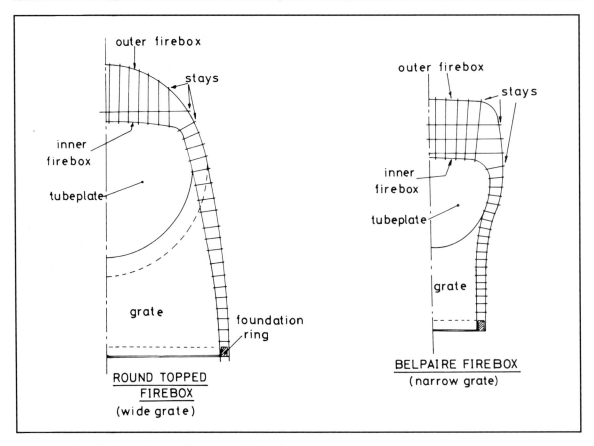

water at the firebox base. Correct width of water leg (the distance between inner and outer firebox) for a particular size of boiler is required to ensure good circulation in the firebox region. Too small a clearance and steam bubbles are not released easily thus restricting water flow, too large a clearance and circulation takes place between inner and outer plates rather than around the firebox. Churchward carried out experiments using vanes within the water legs in order to determine the optimum width for his Belpaire firebox boilers.

Another design feature incorporated to promote better circulation was the Thermic Syphon. Extensively used by Bulleid, but not common to other British locomotives, the arrangement consists of two flattened pipes of triangular form connecting the water space below the firebox front to the section above the firebox. Being in the firebox these syphons are

Diagrams comparing round and Belpaire fireboxes.

subject to intense heat resulting in rapid evaporation of water which they contain. Steam bubbles pass upwards causing more water to be drawn in from below, thus cool water is always taken from the bottom of the boiler giving effective circulation around the firebox. The arrangement provided increased firebox heating surface and could allow for higher boiler evaporation rates although this was never proved in British practice. Welded construction of the syphons gave a clean surface which helped with circulation. Staying was essential and for his 'Leader' Class Bulleid used cross tubes which were welded in place. These not only acted as stays but increased the heat transfer surface area.

Tapered boiler barrels are claimed to have a

number of advantages over parallel barrels for larger boilers. Often tapers are only on the upper part of the boiler, the lower section being parallel with the frames. Because of its reduced diameter less water is retained at the front, cooler, end of the barrel thus allowing a higher evaporation rate from a lower water content boiler. A greater steam space near the firebox can be provided per unit of water held and the taper allows a better view forward for the driver. In some cases the firebox has a slight upwards and outwards slope towards the boiler front. This provides increased firebox and steam space volume as well as making for easier release of steam bubbles.

Steam in as dry a condition as possible, with no water droplets, was always the aim for supply to the cylinders. The regulator valve, which controls steam outlet from the boiler, must always be positioned as high as possible in the steam space. In many cases provision of a dome above the main boiler shell allowed the valve to be placed well clear of the water level. Tall domes could be fitted with smaller boilers

but loading gauge prohibited them with larger locomotives and regulator valves had to be designed which would fit in confined spaces while at the same time allowing the necessary steam flow.

Even with the tallest of domes priming, the carry over of water droplets with the steam, can still take place. In some cases the presence of a dome can make matters worse. Avoidance of priming taxed all locomotive designers and the problem was never fully overcome. High water level is an obvious reason whilst problems related to dissolved salt levels have already been considered. When a regulator valve is opened wide quickly there is a boiler pressure drop near that valve due to steam flowing out. The resulting pressure difference over the boiler length may be very small but reduced pressure does cause water in the vicinity of the regulator to boil more vigorously than elsewhere in the boiler. This is because the water is hotter than the saturation temperature corresponding to that slightly lower pressure. Vigorous boiling results in water droplets passing into the steam flow, producing the priming effect. In order to restrict that problem a number of designers

Arrangement of firebox with thermic syphons.

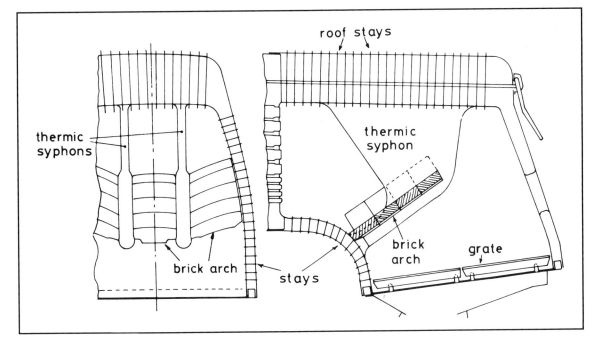

employed perforated steam collectors which spread the steam gathering over a large area thus minimizing any localized pressure drop. Domes tend to concentrate pressure reduction in a very small region resulting in increased risk of priming.

Priming not only causes potential damage problems to cylinders but also results in the formation of scale deposits in the superheater, if fitted. Advantages of superheating will be considered later, for the present only production of superheated steam will be considered. Upon leaving the regulator steam passes to a steam chest and then to a superheater header positioned in the smokebox. Many different designs have been developed but they all consist of elements positioned within the large flue tubes. A superheater element usually comprises a small diameter tube, about 38 mm (1.5 in) diameter, with outward and return legs. In

some types the tube is simply bent in order to provide a return whilst in others special ends are fitted to the tubes. Whatever the arrangement a number of passes are usually provided so that the steam is effectively 'superheated' until it achieves the desired temperature. After its final pass steam returns to the outlet side of the superheater header and thence to the cylinders.

Early superheater systems employed dampers over the ends of the flues and headers in the smokebox in order to prevent hot gases from flowing over the superheater element whenever the regulator was closed. With no cooling steam flow through the elements it was feared that overheating and subsequent failure of elements would take place. Practice showed otherwise as absence of draught prevents gas flow over the elements and later designs simply had superheater headers positioned uncovered

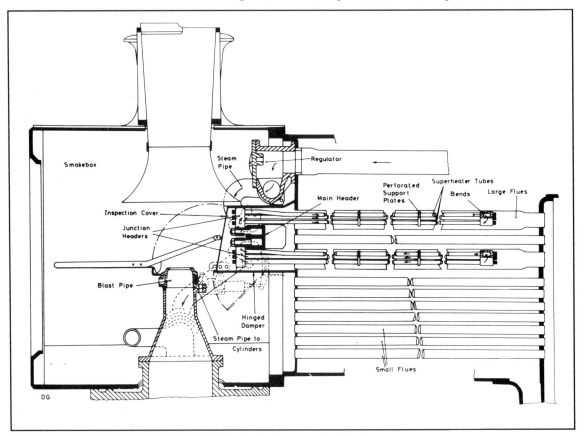

in the smokebox. Slight steam, or air, flow through superheater elements when drifting provides a cooling effect.

The smokebox

In order to promote effective combustion of coal in the firebox it is necessary to have a good air supply. Forced systems employing fans as used in marine and static boilers are not easy to arrange for locomotive operation and so the steam blast form of air induction as fitted in *Rocket* remains. Any steam blast up the chimney will reduce the smokebox pressure and hence allow air to be drawn into the firebox but this needs to be done efficiently.

A correctly designed nozzle (see Appendix) on the blast pipe will produce a high steam velocity and this will draw exhaust gas up the chimney due to the effect of friction. The higher the speed of the steam the greater will be the effect of friction and the larger will be the vacuum obtained within the smokebox. This effect may be observed on the platform of a station through which trains pass at high speed where swirling eddies of wind may occur due to friction between the air and carriage sides.

Correct design of the nozzle and chimney arrangement is essential in order to ensure effective removal of exhaust gas. The jet of steam should touch the chimney sides just before the top of the chimney and so it is essential that a correctly sized nozzle is used to suit the steam condition. The chimney should also be shaped at its lower end in order to allow correct induction of gas flow into the steam jet. Such factors are complex and detailed discussion is beyond the scope of this book.

Production of a high-speed jet of steam requires a sharp nozzle and that results in a

Left *GWR form of superheater arrangement with damper.*

Right *'Castle' Class boiler from smokebox end, showing tubeplate with holes for flues and tubes.*

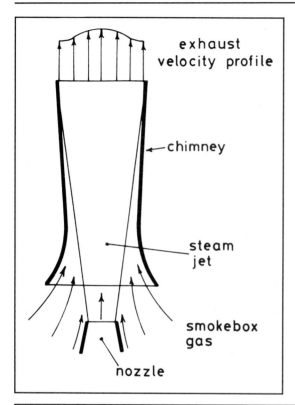

higher back pressure in the steam exhaust line. As may be seen from the section covering cylinder and valve operations a high exhaust back pressure reduces the work obtained from the cylinders. The problem then is one of obtaining an efficient suction effect from the steam jet without producing a high back pressure. At this stage it is worth remembering that the steam locomotive does not operate at exactly the same conditions continuously, nor is the steam supply to the blast a steady flow. Running speed and the number of cylinders dictate the number of exhaust steam blasts per second whilst the nature of operation, load and gradient, will dictate the amount and pressure of exhaust steam. The blast pipe and chimney requirements are, therefore, different for express passenger locomotives and heavy freight locomotives.

Left *Blast pipe jet profile.*

Below *Diagram of Kylchap blast pipe as fitted to LNER 'A4' 'Pacifics'. The anti-vacuum valve may be seen just behind the chimney.*

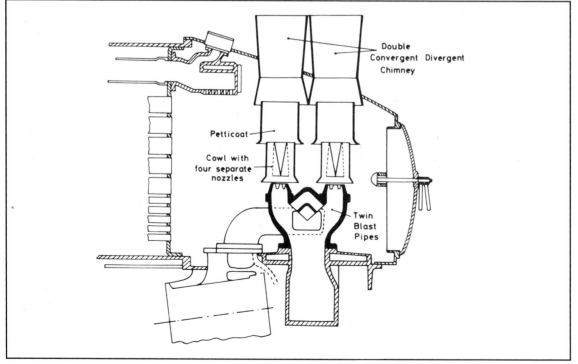

Open casing and smokebox on an 'A4' 'Pacific', with petticoat and cowls just observable.

A single chimney of circular form with a simple blast pipe can be very effective in many instances if properly designed. By contrast for high-speed express locomotives and those working at high loads a number of different systems have been tried over the years with varying degrees of success. The basic requirement of any system is to provide the ideal smokebox vacuum in order to promote good air flow into the firebox but without causing a higher back pressure in the exhaust steam line. High steam velocity from the blast pipe draws gas from the smokebox by means of friction but that only takes place where steam and gas are in contact. The exhaust velocity profile shows how flow is slowed down at the outer surface of the steam jet due to that friction but the middle of the jet just blasts its way up the chimney without taking any gas with it.

A number of designers reached the same conclusion that if the area of contact between steam and gas was increased a high suction effect could be produced resulting in an effective smokebox vacuum. At the same time the steam velocity need not be so high and thus the nozzle area could be enlarged to give a lower back pressure in the steam exhaust line. Different exhaust ejector systems evolved using the principle that a larger number of smaller steam jets give an increased area of contact between steam and gas. In all cases it is essential that each part is properly aligned with others in the system to ensure that the blast goes straight up the chimney.

The Kylchap arrangement, devised by engineers Chapelon and Kylala, comprises twin blast pipes which are each then divided into four separate steam jets by means of four Goodfellow tips in the blast orifice and nozzles in the cowl. Downward chimney extensions, known as petticoats, allow some of the exhaust gas to be drawn into the steam jets at a lower level than the chimney itself. This, and the suction effect on the gas at each blast pipe orifice, helps to obtain a more even drawing action through the boiler tubes, thus giving an even effect on the fire. Double convergent-divergent chimneys further increase the gas suction effect and blast the exhaust clear of the locomotive.

Lemaitre devised an arrangement on similar lines using five separate nozzles on the top of a single blast pipe, these convergent nozzles being inclined outwards at about 1 in 12. An oval-shaped central spear could be raised or lowered to change the central area through the blast pipe and alter the total blast area. This device was well suited to different working conditions. The five main steam jets certainly give a large area of contact but an increased diameter chimney is required. The chimney here takes the convergent-divergent form to ensure gas entrapment. This arrangement of exhaust ejector system found favour with Bulleid and was used in modified form for the Southern Railway's 'Lord Nelson', 'Q1' and 'Pacific' Classes.

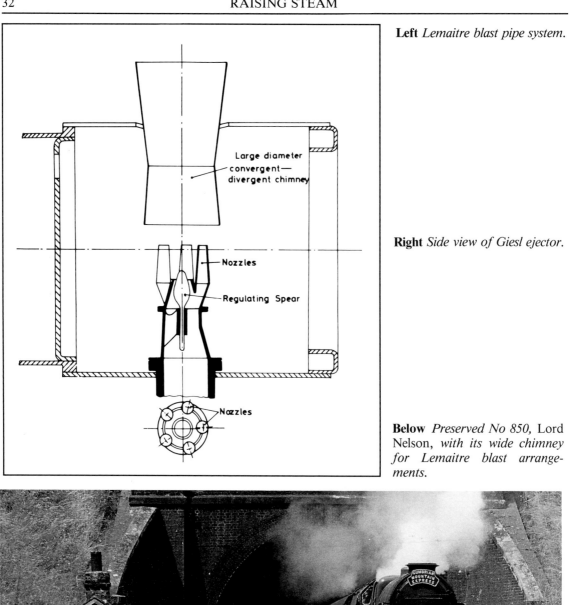

Large diameter
convergent—
divergent chimney

Nozzles

Regulating Spear

Nozzles

Left *Lemaitre blast pipe system.*

Right *Side view of Giesl ejector.*

Below *Preserved No 850,* Lord Nelson, *with its wide chimney for Lemaitre blast arrangements.*

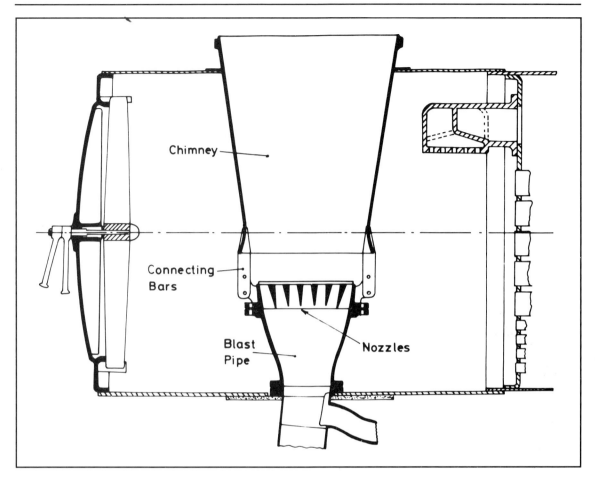

The above smokebox arrangements had widespread use but another, the Giesl ejector, came too late in the steam era to receive thorough testing. Its potential, however, is often considered to be greater than that of the other forms. It too makes use of multiple steam nozzles but they are arranged in line at the top of a single blast pipe. These nozzles are actually rectangular and the area can be changed to suit different conditions, by lateral movement of two steel strips. Seven separate jets give an enlarged area of gas contact and so improve the draught. The narrow frontal area of the chimney offers reduced wind resistance to the escaping exhaust which is at a high velocity due to the design of ejector. These factors result in the exhaust being lifted well clear of the locomotive.

Most ejector systems, however, only truly suit a narrow range of exhaust steam conditions. If the locomotive operates for most of its time within that range then the design can be considered satisfactory and the slight loss in performance which must exist at other times can be tolerated. If, however, the locomotive must operate regularly with different loads and speeds on varying gradients then problems can occur. On the GWR it was found that large freight locomotives operating at cut-offs in excess of 40 per cent produced very sharp blasts because of the high exhaust steam pressure. Blast velocity produced increased vacuum conditions in the smokebox resulting in an excessive draught which pulled the fire apart.

The solution devised was a jumper-top blast pipe. At small cut-offs, below 40 per cent,

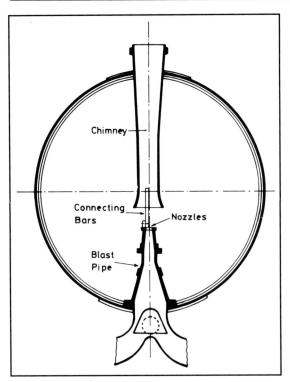

Above *Front view of Giesl ejector and chimney.*

Below *GWR jumper top blast pipe.*

Above *Giesl chimney as fitted to the 'West Country' 'Pacific' City of Wells.*

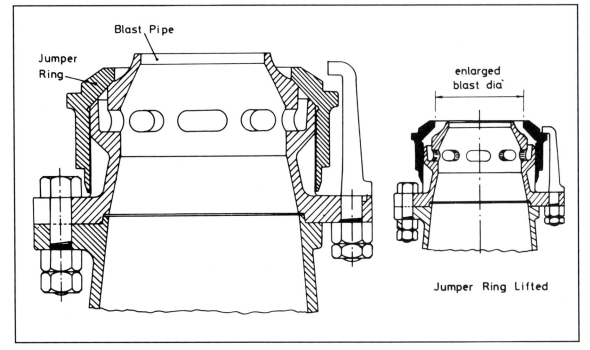

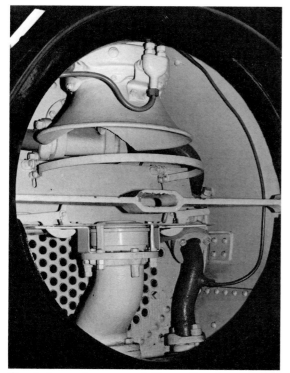

Smokebox of preserved Dean Goods No 2516 showing jumper-top blast pipe.

exhaust steam pressure is relatively low and the jumper ring remains in its seated position allowing the normal blast pipe area to apply. At greater cut-offs exhaust pressure is higher and steam, passing through radial holes in the blast pipe, acts upon the jumper ring causing it to lift, increasing the effective blast pipe area and thus reducing jet velocity and weakening the draught.

With all ejector systems correct design of nozzle and chimney is essential to achieve effective performance. The theory of smokebox design is very involved but these examples show how different systems have been devised to satisfy the somewhat conflicting requirements of good smokebox vacuum and low steam back pressure. Defects such as a badly fitting smokebox door, however, will allow air into the smokebox thereby destroying the vacuum and blast effect of any system.

When a locomotive is standing it is fre-

quently necessary to liven up a fire but without the assistance of any exhaust blast because the cylinders are not working. In these circumstances a blower exists on steam locomotives to provide such a blast. In basic terms the blower consists of a steam pipe, about 25 mm (1 in), diameter wrapped circumferentially around the outside of the blast pipe. The pipe has a number of small holes facing upwards or it may be fitted with a number of jet nozzles. When steam is applied to the pipe it is directed upwards by the holes or nozzles providing a continuous steam jet. This acts in the same way as a jet issuing from the blast pipe although it is not as strong. Correct design in terms of number of holes and spread of jet stream will give an efficient blower system. Efficiency however, is not as critical as it is with a blast pipe because the blower only operates infrequently and does not exert a back pressure on the cylinders.

A blower in operation may be observed at any preserved steam railway by its visual and audible effects. A locomotive using its blower while standing at a platform end issues a distinctive and lively exhaust from its chimney with steam also being visible during cold or wet weather. Although used for livening up a fire of a locomotive at rest the blower may also be employed to safeguard against firebox blowback during coasting with the steam shut off. Under certain conditions the lack of smokebox blast can result in a back pressure acting down the tubes which may cause fire to enter the cab through the firehole. Using the blower at such times prevents the risk but relies upon the skill and knowledge of the driver and fireman in understanding the situation.

Even with a good blast system there will always be carry-over of char, unburnt particles of coal, and sparks to the smokebox. Sparks can have the effect of igniting lineside grass and crops during dry summer conditions and during the days of BR steam operations many legal battles were waged regarding compensation. There was never any requirement in Britain that spark arresters be fitted to locomotives although the practice was common overseas. Despite this a number of British designers did make use of spark arresters with self-cleaning smokeboxes and the use of such a device has often allowed a preserved locomotive to undertake a mainline outing during periods of fire risk when locomotives not so fitted have been barred.

The type of spark-arresting self-cleaning smokebox which found favour for BR standard locomotives and was also subsequently fitted to other classes, comprises a sloping baffle over the tube plate which serves to deflect the gases downwards and increase velocity. A wire mesh screen is positioned in front of the blast pipe and through this the gases pass to the chimney. The mesh breaks up the larger particles of char allowing only small particles to be ejected through the chimney with the blast. The action of breaking up larger particles reduces the incidence of lineside fires as the fine particles which are ejected burn out before they fall back to earth. A simpler arrangement fitted to some locomotives, including former GWR 'Kings', consists of a wire mesh cage which surrounds the blast pipe.

Towards the end of the 19th century the London & North Western Railway fitted its newer locomotives with a steam-operated device for cleaning the smokebox whilst in service. It simply consisted of a perforated steam pipe in the bottom of the smokebox through which steam would be directed by the fireman as required. Char became agitated, was caught up in the blast and directed up the chimney. This simple device never found favour elsewhere and subsequently fell out of use on the host railway.

Self cleaning smokeboxes reduced the need for manual cleaning but its anti-social aspects did not find favour with everybody, many lineside housewives having their washday efforts ruined by the descending dust. Slight draughting modifications had to be made to locomotives fitted with such systems in order to

Right *Blower operating principle.*

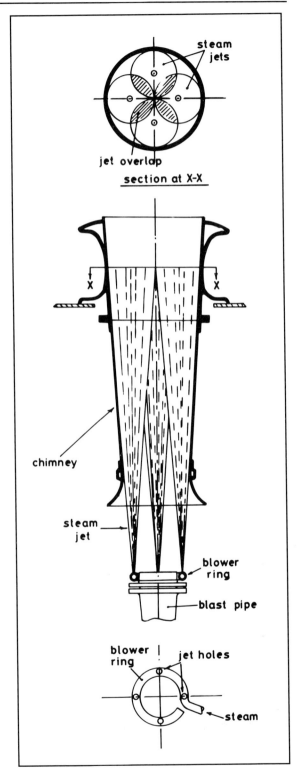

overcome the additional resistance produced by the baffles and mesh screens. Char building up in a smokebox will reduce its volume thus impairing draught effectiveness and steaming capability. Burning of the char can also occur, especially after a period of hard running, the evidence of this being a scorched smokebox door. Benefits of manual or self cleaning of smokeboxes should now be evident but for the short runs operated on preserved lines there are fewer problems than existed in active steam days.

Smoke deflectors are fitted to some steam locomotives and not others for the not illogical reason that there is a need in some cases and not others! These appendages at the smokebox sides encourage chimney exhaust to be thrown high enough to clear the cab and avoid obscuring the driver's view. Shaped and positioned for optimum effect, deflectors direct the air flow at a locomotive's front end along the boiler sides and upwards thus minimizing the likelihood of smoke drifting down over the cab. Despite wind tunnel testing deflectors and boiler front design failed to prevent the problem with Bulleid's 'Pacific' locomotives. Only the fitting of a Giesl ejector which threw the exhaust high seems to have overcome the nuisance with these machines. Operating tender, or bunker, first avoided the drifting smoke problem. Garratt locomotives, in Britain and elsewhere, were sometimes worked cab first for this reason and because the smoke always remained behind the cab whilst passing through tunnels.

The suitability of smoke deflectors for a particular locomotive depended upon blast and chimney arrangement, shape of boiler front, boiler length and numerous unknowns such as the speed of the locomotive as well as the direction and speed of any wind. In most cases designers got the things right, even if a number of modifications were required to achieve that end.

Before leaving discussion of the boiler structure it is worth considering lagging and cladding. In simple terms cladding consists of sheets of thin steel plate which hold the lagging in place. It is the cladding which is painted and lined out in attractive colours, not the boiler shell itself. Lagging, or insulation, is there to conserve heat just as it is with any domestic hot water cylinder. There is no difference in purpose it's just that a lined-out boiler looks more attractive than a cylinder jacket. Asbestos, used extensively years ago, is now banned and other forms of insulation such as fibreglass and rockwool blankets are employed. A good layer of insulation around the boiler shell and firebox, but not the smokebox, prevents heat loss with its corresponding reduction in efficiency.

Preserved 'King Arthur' Class 4-6-0 Sir Lamiel, bearing smokebox door scorch marks following a period of hard work — the simple smoke deflectors may also be seen.

Boiler mountings

A working boiler is potentially dangerous as it contains a highly expansive mixture of pressurized hot water and steam. Failure of any part can lead to a catastrophic explosion but good design and construction minimize the risk within pressure limits for which the boiler has been designed: only higher than expected pressure may lead to failure. Tight regulations invariably govern the design and construction of pressure vessels such as boilers and insist upon satisfactory measures to prevent overpressure, namely safety valves. Ordinary spring-loaded safety valves are designed to lift at a set pressure, release steam from the boiler and thus prevent overload but they suffer from one serious disadvantage. Spring setting is adjusted by means of a screw thread allowing the valve to lift at that set pressure but as the valve lifts to release steam it compresses the spring, increasing the valve loading: the steam pressure must then increase before the valve can lift further. As a result the valves are always set below maximum boiler pressure.

Ross 'pop' valves were designed to overcome the problem. The valve is still spring-loaded, but lifting pressure is set by means of spring tension which results from the top casing being screwed onto the body. A setting ring of particular thickness limits the amount by which the top casing can be screwed down. When steam pressure causes the valve to lift some steam can escape through holes in the valve lip and this causes the characteristic 'pop'. It also increases the effective valve area allowing more steam to escape for the same amount of valve lift. Steam escapes from the outlet holes in the cover, the area of these holes being adjustable to suit the desired steam loss rate. At least two valves are always required for each boiler, the size of these being dictated by the size of boiler,

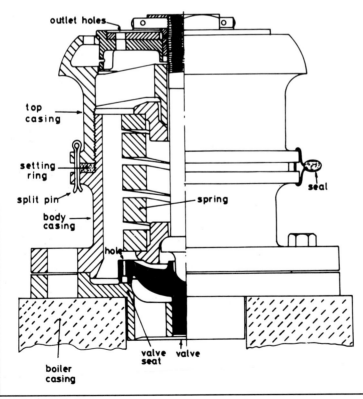

Left *Ross 'pop' safety valve.*

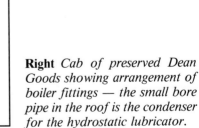

Right *Cab of preserved Dean Goods showing arrangement of boiler fittings — the small bore pipe in the roof is the condenser for the hydrostatic lubricator.*

its maximum evaporation rate and steam pressure. Valves are nominally set at the same pressure but will tend to lift at slightly different pressures because of slight variations in setting. It is essential that valves are sealed following setting and tampering is prevented.

Maintenance of water level within the boiler is essential to safe operation (as already discussed) and so a means of determining that level is necessary. Two independent water gauge glasses are usually provided for the purpose but where only one gauge glass is fitted a set of test cocks will allow the approximate level of the water to be determined. A gauge glass is positioned so that normal water level shows at mid-point in the glass and it connects with steam and water spaces by means of cocks. The gauge glass tube is actually held in upper and lower housing by means of gland nuts, the glands being packed to prevent leakage. A drain cock is also provided at the lower glass housing. During normal service steam and water cocks are open with the drain closed, allowing the glass to indicate water level in the boiler.

Periodically the glass should be blown in order to ensure that it is giving the correct reading since restricted cock passages can provide a false level. Blowing through simply consists of opening the drain whilst closing and then opening steam and water cocks in turn. Reading the water level can be difficult and some operators fitted cards with striped lines behind the glass, the refraction of glass and water changing the angle of those stripes where water was present. The later reflex type of enclosed gauge overcame the problem by use of a prismatic glass sheet at the rear of the gauge block.

The reflex gauge also prevents the risk of injury resulting from a broken gauge glass tube because it comprises a metal block with thick glass sheets instead of tubes. Tube type gauges are normally fitted with glass guards to minimize the risk of injury to footplate crew from fragments of glass should a tube break. In the event of such breakage steam and water flow are restricted by means of ball valves in upper and lower housing allowing fireman or driver to safely shut the cocks.

The other essential item to ensure safety is the pressure gauge and again, very often, two are fitted. The danger of overpressure should be prevented by the safety valves but if the safety valves are stuck for any reason then the pressure gauge should provide a warning. During the last century it was not unknown for a driver to screw down the safety valves in order to increase maximum steam pressure and so get increased performance from his machine. A number of boiler explosions were attributable to such malpractice. Pressure gauges, although fitted as a safety feature, are also a valuable aid to driver and fireman in operating the locomotive allowing the fireman in particular to regulate his firing and water feed in order to keep the required steam pressure and water level. Safety valves provide protection but if they have to operate water and coal are wasted.

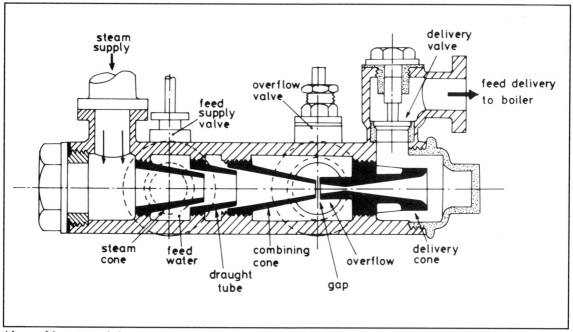

Above Live steam injector.
Below left *A pair of live steam injectors on a BR standard Class '4MT' loco.*

Injectors

A supply of water to the boiler is essential for safe steam generation and to achieve this the water pressure must be raised above that existing within the boiler. Earliest locomotives employed crankshaft driven pumps supplemented by hand pumps for initial filling. Subsequent arrangements made use of steam-driven reciprocating pumps but, following its invention by Henri Giffard in 1859, the injector became popular in Britain and remained so until the end of steam traction. A number of variations were developed during the steam era but they all operated on the same basic principles and so it is unnecessary to detail them. Common to all types was the nozzle, or rather the effect of several nozzles.

The live steam injector diagram above illustrates the essential features of operation. Steam from a supply valve has its velocity increased during passage through the steam cone, the speed being in the region of 500 metres per second. This velocity ensures that feed water is drawn into the draught tube and mixes with the high-speed steam. Partial condensation of the steam occurs in the combining cone and the resultant suction effect means more water is drawn through. Both effects result in the steam being able to force about twelve times its own mass of water through the combining cone at a speed of about 40 metres per second. This velocity is sufficient to carry the flow across the gap to the convergent-divergent delivery cone. In the diverging part of the delivery cone velocity energy is converted into pressure energy resulting in a pressure rise sufficient to allow water feed to be delivered to the boiler through the clack valves. Should steam flow be insufficient or water flow excessive the velocity reached in the combining cone will not carry the flow across the gap and overflow will take place. An excessive steam flow would result in some steam flowing to the delivery cone where it would expand in the divergent section producing a velocity but not a pressure increase. This would then cause a build up in back pressure and, again an over-

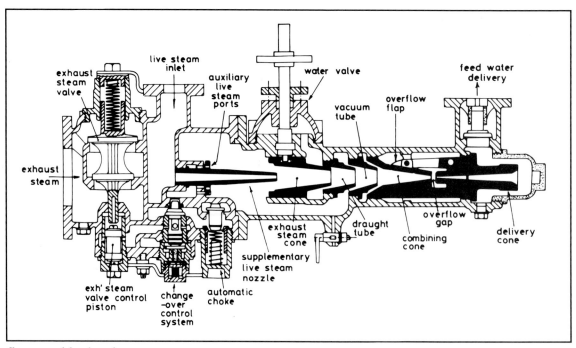

Exhaust steam injector.

flow would take place.

The exhaust steam injector uses the same principles but the whole arrangement is rather more complex in operation. Because exhaust steam is employed and this has less pressure and heat energy, the cones are designed for increased steam flow. A small supply of live steam is used in order to ensure that the correct pressure is reached, supply of this live steam being under the control of an automatic system actuated by the exhaust steam pressure. The automatic system also changes over to live steam operation whenever the regulator is closed and back again when it is opened. As may be seen from the diagram above the control system consists of a number of valve units but its operation is very involved and beyond the scope of this book.

As far as the nozzle systems are concerned the action is almost identical to the live steam injector except that more nozzles are employed to produce the correct velocity for the higher mass of steam flowing. The type shown has a hinged overflow flap forming part of the combining cone and this will open to release any excess steam or water which occurs due to a

build up of pressure in that section due to increased water or steam flow. When conditions return to normal the flap closes and operation resumes.

The fireman must ensure that he regulates steam and water flows to the injectors in order to obtain the correct feed rate. Skill is required but a 'singing' injector is music for it guarantees that water is being fed to the boiler. The 'singing' or whistling sound is the result of steam condensation in the cones: a similar effect may be heard just before a kettle boils as the steam bubbles condense before they reach the surface of the water.

Because it makes use of a large mass of steam the exhaust steam injector also acts as a feed water heater and thereby improves overall boiler efficiency by up to 10 per cent: it also saves on water since less steam passes up the chimney.

An indispensable fitting for use with an exhaust steam injector is the grease separator. Lubrication of the cylinders, essential with superheated steam, introduces oil to the steam system and some of this, naturally, passes with the steam to the exhaust steam injector. Any oil entering a boiler is detrimental in that it produces an insulating layer on heat transfer surfaces, increases acidity which tends to cause corrosion and modifies some of the salts so that they produce a hard scale. In order to avoid the problem a grease separator is fitted in the exhaust steam line to the injectors.

The simplest form is that devised by Davies and Metcalfe where a twisted vane at the inlet end of the separator chamber gives the incoming exhaust steam a swirling action. The heavier water and oil particles are flung outwards against the separator walls by centrifugal force whilst the much lighter steam passes around a baffle plate in the chamber centre to the outlet pipe. The baffle prevents ash from entering the injector, water and oil drain from the walls to the chamber bottom and are removed via an automatic drip valve. Only pure exhaust steam, therefore, passes to the injector.

Clack valves, mounted on the boiler shell, allow feed water into the boiler. The positioning of these valves depends upon the designer but they are most frequently fitted on the first

Arrangement of exhaust steam injector and water pipes on a Southern Railway 'Lord Nelson' Class locomotive.

ring, that boiler section immediately behind the smokebox, or at the top of the barrel where 'top feed' is considered to be most suitable. Each position has advantages: at the front end cold feed is introduced to the cooler part of the boiler thus minimizing thermal stress problems, whilst top feed with a delivery tray allows for a degree of feed heating upon entry. Clack valves are spring-loaded so that they give an effective non-return action; valves close as soon as feed pressure falls below boiler pressure thus preventing steam from flowing back out of the delivery line.

Regulators

Once steam has been generated its passage to the cylinders, by way of a superheater if fitted, must be controlled and that is the purpose of the regulating valve. In most cases a regulator is situated in the boiler at the dome but in the case of domeless GWR-designed boilers, and BR standard 'Pacifics' for example the regulator is mounted in the smokebox at the superheater header. No matter which form is used the regulator is basically a variable-opening valve under control of the driver, which controls the quantity of steam which may flow and hence the steam pressure which will exist in the valve chests of the cylinders (see Chapter 3). Because of pipe resistance valve chest pressure will

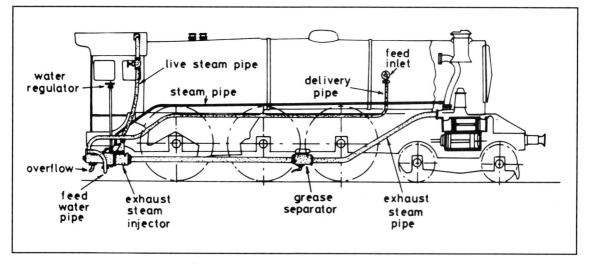

always be lower than boiler pressure but the regulator may also be used as a means of obtaining an even lower pressure at delivery to the cylinders. As will be discussed later many drivers use a combination of steam pressure and cylinder steam cut-off for controlling locomotive power.

The balanced regulator employed by many LNER locomotives has two seating faces and the design requires very little force to open or close. This is because, as the name implies, downward steam forces on the valve are balanced by upward forces and the regulator control only has to overcome the weight of the valve and friction in the linkages. Lifting of the valve from its seats allows steam flow to the cylinders.

The LMS pattern of regulator comprises two sliding valves on a flat seat with ports in the valves and seat. An operating pin, moved by a

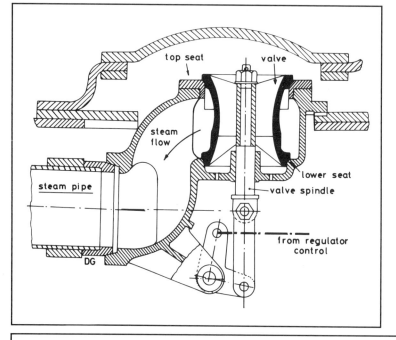

Left *LNER pattern balanced regulator.*

Below *LMS pattern regulator.*

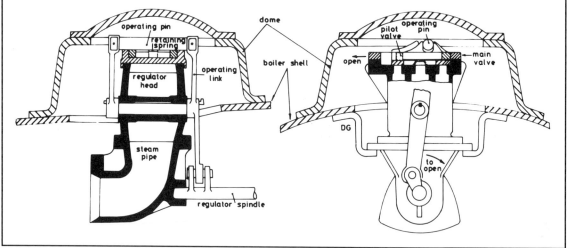

lever from the regulator spindle, engages with slots in lugs which project above the valves causing sideways movement of the valve when the regulator handle is moved. Initial movement of the operating pin first moves the pilot or starting valve to uncover starting ports in the main valve and seat. This allows a reduced flow of steam to the cylinders because of the restricted area of the starting ports. When the starting ports are fully uncovered the design is such that the operating pin will have moved sufficiently to contact slots in the main valve, moving it and thereby opening the three main ports in the valve seat. A flat retaining spring keeps the pilot valve firmly on the main valve.

When drifting or running downhill without steam applied for power, some steam is usually allowed to flow to the valve chest and cylinders. This is to avoid the risk of gases and ash entering the steam side of the system through the blast pipe because there is no pressure at the steam chest. Considerable damage can result from ash wearing on the cylinder and reducing the effectiveness of cylinder lubrication. In most cases regulators are provided with a 'drifting' position which allows a small amount of steam to the valve chest. With LMS-type regulators the pilot valve is partly open for drifting, the regulator handle being fitted with a spring-loaded catch so that the handle will stay in that position. This also allows for a cooling steam flow to the superheater element.

In many cases the operating spindles for the regulator pass through the boiler steam space from the firebox back plate but in others, BR standard classes in particular, an operating link passes along the boiler side and the spindle enters the boiler shell by means of a gland. (BR standard 'Pacifics' with regulators at the superheater header had spindles entering the smokebox by way of a gland.) With the latter types regulator levers are controlled in a fore and aft direction whilst with the former the lever is moved sideways across the cab.

Other fittings are provided on boilers but these will be discussed later. We have now considered the boiler in general terms although particular examples have been used to illustrate usual practice. It should be remembered that many variations exist in the construction of boilers and mountings but this outline should have enabled the reader to obtain a reasonable understanding of the locomotive boiler without having to worry about technical details or the finer points of construction.

CHAPTER 3

Cylinders and power generation

Steam acting on the face of a piston in a cylinder forces that piston down the cylinder: such is the action of the simple steam engine. By means of a crosshead, connecting rod and crank the moving piston may be made to rotate a shaft allowing useful work to be produced. If the shaft has wheels attached to it then we have possibilities for locomotion. Leaving the matter like that might satisfy some railway enthusiasts who believe that going any deeper requires a thorough knowledge of engineering but this is not the case. Certainly in design there is a need for technical understanding, but to appreciate the workings of the steam engine side of a locomotive only enthusiasm is essential and I hope that the text which follows will supply the basic detail. The engine part, with its flashing rods, animated linkages and blurred wheels, is the most visually stimulating of any locomotive.

Steam locomotive cylinders are double-acting which means that steam first acts on one side of the piston forcing it down the cylinder then more steam is made to act on the other face to push the piston back up the cylinder. (Use of the words 'up' and 'down' do not necessarily signify that the cylinder is vertical it is merely convention to refer to the end of the cylinder which has no opening for the piston rod as the top.) Whilst steam forces the piston one way the action on the opposite side is for exhaust to take place and the piston forces 'used' or exhaust steam out of the cylinder. An important point to consider at this stage is that the higher the exhaust or back pressure the greater the amount of work which must be used from the other side of the piston in forcing that exhaust steam out. Good design requires that exhaust steam flows freely from the cylinder through valve openings as large as possible and through a blast pipe which offers the minimum resistance.

Let us look then at one complete stroke of the piston, down and up the cylinder, making reference to what happens on one side only. Steam is not allowed to enter the cylinder for the whole of the stroke, that would be wasteful of steam and cause problems on the exhaust side, especially at the blast pipe. For a certain portion of the stroke steam admission takes place. This ceases at a 'cut-off point', the amount of cut-off referring to the percentage of the piston stroke during which steam enters the cylinder: a 60 per cent cut-off means that steam is admitted to the cylinder for 60 per cent of its stroke. The amount of cut-off is an indication of the amount of steam being used, higher cut-offs using more steam per piston stroke than lower cut-offs.

After cut-off, steam in the cylinder expands, giving up its energy as it forces the piston down the cylinder until release and the commencement of exhaust occurs. The point at which release takes place has to be carefully calculated, too early and useful work is lost: too late and all of the steam cannot escape effectively thus imposing a back pressure against the piston when it begins to move in the opposite direction. After release the piston is still moving downwards to the botton of its stroke and steam escapes from the cylinder. Some work is still obtained as that escaping steam has a pressure higher than that existing on the opposite side of the piston.

As the piston is forced back up the cylinder residual steam on the top side is forced out until at a certain point in the stroke the exhaust valve closes, preventing further steam escape. Remaining steam is compressed providing a cushion effect which avoids knock when steam is again admitted to that side of the piston. The steam valve actually opens before the piston reaches the end of its upward stroke, this is known as valve 'lead'. This may seem a strange thing to do but allowing the steam valve to open early permits full steam pressure to build up in the cylinder by the time the piston reaches the end of its stroke.

Although the sight of steam escaping from safety valves may give the impression that its action is instantaneous, this is far from the case and the faster an engine operates the longer it takes in terms of piston movement for steam to flow through passageways to the cylinder. The situation is similar to that of the car or motorcycle engine which requires an ignition timing advance mechanism to compensate for the fact that ignition of fuel takes a set period of time and the faster the engine goes the further the piston moves in that time. Stephenson valve gear actually varies the amount of lead as cut-off is changed. Churchward preferred Stephenson gear for that reason, allowing him to set a + 3 mm (0.125 in) at 25 per cent cut-off with − 3 mm in full gear, maximum cut-off. The negative amount when starting caused no problems whilst at 25 per cent cut-off a locomotive would be expected to be running at speed and that 3 mm lead provided the perfect effect.

At different values of cut-off different quantities of steam are used but the amount of work

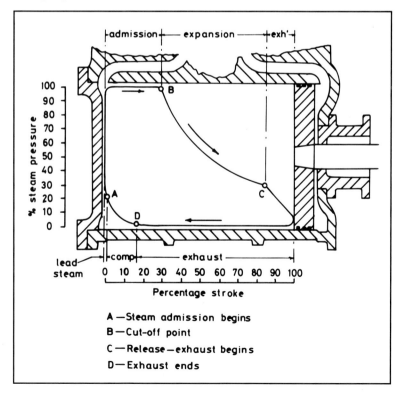

Cylinder steam events.

obtained from the cylinder does not change to the same extent because of 'expansive' working. A 70 per cent cut-off is the maximum generally used with British locomotives although if steam is admitted for 70 per cent of the stroke it leaves very little time available for

Cylinder pressure – volume diagram for different cut-offs.

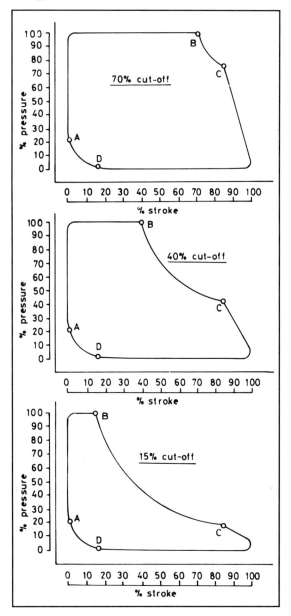

the steam to expand before release. A considerable amount of work, represented by the area of the pressure/volume diagram, can be obtained at this value of cut-off but it is at the expense of steam consumption. In addition the high pressure at release can cause problems with the blast and most expansive energy in the steam is used up in the blast pipe or goes to forming attractive steam patterns in the atmosphere.

At reduced cut-off, say 40 per cent, less work is obtained but less steam is consumed because greater use is made of the steam's expansive properties. At 15 per cent cut-off, not normally used in practice, the lowest usually being about 25 per cent, a very small amount of steam is employed but considerable energy is gained from its expansion. It has to be remembered that each cylinder is double acting with work being obtained as the piston moves in each direction.

Thus the work produced in a cylinder not only relates to the amount of steam allowed in but also upon the degree to which that steam is allowed to expand before exhaust commences. The cut-off value employed in operation depends upon the amount of work required from the cylinders, which in turn is governed by load, gradient and speed. In working practice both cut-off and steam chest pressure, controlled by the amount of regulator opening, are used by most drivers to control the power output of their charge. A lower steam pressure at inlet may be used with large cut-off without producing severe blast which can destroy the fire. In simple terms, for the same steam inlet pressure the larger the value of cut-off the greater the amount of work developed but the higher the steam comsumption. In general large cut-offs are used when starting or hauling heavy loads up inclines, whilst small cut-offs can be employed with fast trains on the level or on easy grades.

Superheating

When steam enters a cylinder some may condense upon the relatively cold cylinder walls

Steam today

Above *Preserved LMS 2-8-0 '8F' No 8233 at Bewdley with a demonstration freight train.*
Below *Sectioned rebuilt 'Merchant Navy' Class locomotive* Ellerman Lines *on display at the National Railway Museum, York.*

Left *The open cab is seen on the antique locomotive* Bellerophon *as she leaves Keighley.*

Below left *South African Class '25NC' No 3425,* Trixie, *blows down her boiler as she heads south near Potfontein on the Kimberley to De Aar line.*

Bottom left *South African Class '25' condensing locomotive No 3511 at Kimberley.*

Top right *LNER 'K4' Class locomotive* The Great Marquess *under restoration at Bridgnorth. The unclad boiler, cab and draw gear may easily be seen.*

Above *GMAM Garrat No 4072 heads away from Oudtshoorn for a trip over the notorious Montague Pass.*

Right *Shed scene in preservation. Ropley, on the Mid-Hants Railway, as No 34105 and No 31806 are prepared for a day's work.*

Above *Streamlined 'A4' No 4498,* Sir Nigel Gresley, *approaches Wennington tunnel.*

Left Flying Scotsman *leaves Southport with an excursion to Manchester in 1987. Wide grate, round top firebox, banjo shaped steam collector and anti-vacuum valve behind the chimney may be seen.*

Left *BR standard tank No 80079 at work on the Severn Valley Railway.*

Right *American style. Transportation Corp 2-8-0 'S160' Class No 5820 at Keighley.*

Below *Bridgnorth yard in the early morning. The stylings of GWR 'City' 4-4-0* City of Truro, *LMS Ivatt 2-6-0 No 43106 and LMS 'Jubilee'* Leander *may be compared.*

Above *Urie 'S15' Class 4–6–0 No 506, beautifully restored, on the Mid-Hants Railway.*

Left *Austerity 2–10–0 No 90775 at Arlesford on the Mid-Hants Railway.*

Right *Standard class '4MT' No 75078 climbs out of Keighley.*

Right *Ivatt design Class '2MT' 2-6-4 tank No 41241 with a passenger train on the Worth Valley Railway.*

Below *A 'Manor' undressed. Foxcote Manor without boiler cladding illustrates what a boiler actually looks like.*

Above *GWR 'Manor' Class No 7819,* Hinton Manor, *prepares to leave Bewdley for Kidderminster during December 1987.*

Left City of Truro, *perhaps the most famous 4-4-0 locomotive ever to turn a wheel.*

Below *No 47383. A typical 'Jinty' 0-6-0 which served the LMS and BR as shunters and branch line locomotives.*

thus preventing it from giving up useful work and requiring more steam to be supplied in order to take its place. Condensation may also take place during expansion depending upon circumstances, but in both cases useful work is lost. Condensation takes place because steam gives up its heat to the colder surface just as steam in a bathroom condenses on cold window and tiled surfaces. This is the latent heat which had to be supplied in order to provide evaporation. Careful lagging of cylinder walls minimizes heat loss to the atmosphere but cylinder walls are inevitably cooled during expansion on the previous piston stroke.

Superheating steam causes its temperature to rise above the saturation temperature corresponding to a given pressure and so some degree of cooling can take place before the steam is cooled back to the point where condensation will take place. Thus superheating avoids cylinder condensation and so avoids the loss of work due to it. A further advantage possessed by superheated steam is that its unit mass occupies a greater volume than saturated steam at the same pressure which means that less steam is required for each piston stroke. Steam, and hence water, consumption is therefore reduced.

Saturated steam at a pressure of 15 bar or $1,500kN/m^2$ (217.5 psi) has a temperature of 198.3°C (338.9°F), each kilogram occupying $0.1317 m^3$ ($4.64 ft^3$). At 300°C (572°F) each kilogram of steam occupies $0.1697 m^3$ ($5.98 ft^3$) thus one kilogram of superheated steam can be used for more strokes of the piston at the same degree of cut-off.

It has been claimed that savings in the region of 25 per cent can be achieved from superheating, mostly due to the avoidance of condensation, but some of the saving is also obtained from the fact that less steam is needed for the same amount of work, thus saving coal. Superheating allows for a reduction in boiler size for a given load because more energy is contained in each unit mass of steam and more of that energy is recovered in the cylinder. These factors allow a reduction in boiler pressure without reducing engine power and many designers took this option with the introduction of superheating. Lower boiler pressure allows for a reduction in maintenance costs and increased operating life and smaller boilers use less water per mile of travel.

From the above it would appear that superheating is all gain but there are prices to pay. The capital and maintenance costs of superheater elements needs to be considered: in addition there is the problem of lubrication in the engine cylinders. Saturated steam always contains some water which acts as a lubricant for the valve and piston rings but superheated steam is dry and excessive wear can result if the means are not provided for lubrication of these parts. Different types of cylinder lubricators have been designed over the years and they all supply oil to the steam chest in measured quantities. This overcomes the lubrication problem but introduces another in that (as discussed on page 42) oil must be removed from the exhaust steam before it may be used in an exhaust steam injector. Who says steam locomotives are simple?

An effective steam side lubricator must introduce oil against pressure and a number of different designs have been developed. The Wakefield mechanical lubricator proved effective with many locomotives, whilst the hydrostatic lubricator also found favour with some railways especially Southern and GWR. Mechanical lubricators, which may be used for the lubrication of bearings and slide bars as well as cylinders, consist of a number of single or double-acting pumps housed in a single box which contains a supply of oil. The pumps are actuated by a ratchet linkage driven from a suitable engine point such as the crosshead allowing oil to be supplied whenever the engine operates. Such lubricator boxes may be observed on the running plate of a locomotive.

On LMS-designed locomotives oil for lubricating cylinders and stuffing boxes is supplied directly via back pressure or non-return valves but oil for lubricating the steam chest is supplied via an atomizer. Here steam and oil

Left *Crosshead and cylinder of an LMS 'Pacific', showing slide bar lubricators and mechanical cylinder lubricator on the running plate.*

Below *Superheated steam cylinder and valve chests showing lubricating oil connection.*

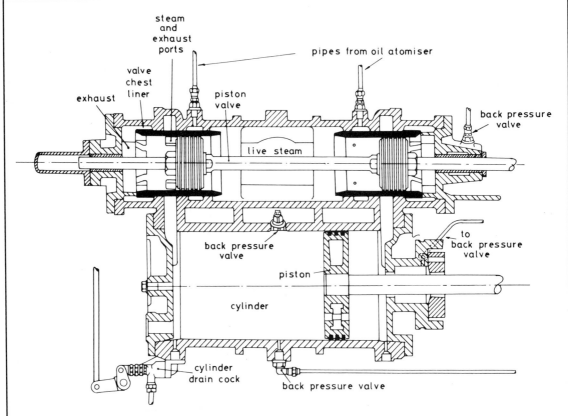

from each pump outlet are intimately mixed by a swirling action induced by the shape of each chamber before being delivered to an outlet connection. The mixture passes to points in the steam chest directly, the absence of back pressure valves allowing oil to enter through a number of small holes drilled in the steam chest liners. An even oil supply is then distributed to the piston valves by the main steam flow itself. A system of levers connected with cylinder drain cocks only allows oil to the atomizer when the drain cocks are closed.

Hydrostatic lubricators work on the principle that condensed steam entering a reservoir displaces oil which will then flow to outlets feeding the cylinder points. Fittings are placed in the cab and consist of a sight-glass-fitted displacement lubricator, steam fountain and condensing coil. Steam is taken from the fountain and enters two spiral coils fitted to the roof of the cab, these coils acting as condensers. Water from the coils passes to the lubricator thus displacing oil, the flow of which may be observed in the sight glasses. An outlet from the lubricator is taken directly to the smokebox for lubricating the regulator whilst those for cylinder lubrication pass to the lubricator control valve having first been mixed with steam coming from the fountain. This control valve is operated by a linkage connected with the regulator, thus lubrication supply is controlled by regulator opening.

Cylinder drain cocks are essential in order to allow for the removal of condensed steam when starting the engine. Water is virtually incompressible and could cause serious damage if it remained in the cylinder. The presence of water due to priming has the same effect. Drain cocks, controlled by rods and levers from the footplate, are fitted in the lowest part of the cylinders to allow for water removal. Spring-loaded relief valves allow for the automatic release of trapped water and in many cases combined relief and drain valves are provided for cylinders.

A further essential fitting for cylinder protection is the anti-vacuum valve which is designed to prevent the formation of a vacuum in the cylinder when the locomotive is drifting with steam shut off. With non-superheated steam engines these would be placed on the cylinder or steam chest but for superheated engines they were usually placed on the saturated steam side of the superheater header. Use of 'drifting' steam (a small flow through the system) avoids the problems but valves were often fitted as added protection, LMS and GWR locomotives usually being fitted with cylinder anti-vacuum valves in addition to those on superheater headers. A cylinder vacuum, as already discussed, could result in ash being drawn into the cylinders the instant a regulator was closed, thus causing excessive wear. Such a vacuum may also exert a braking effect on the locomotive in that its formation consumes energy.

Lack of steam passing through the superheater tubes could result in overheating but if some air is allowed to circulate through them burning can be avoided. In practice there is little risk of superheater tubes burning as gas flow through the flue tubes is very slight when coasting but the air circulation provides a safeguard. Use of drifting steam avoids all of these potential problems and was sometimes adopted in Britain although not generally worldwide.

The prevention of leakage from the ends of cylinders and valve chests through which the rods pass is essential for efficient performance. Packed glands using tallow-soaked hemp rings provided effective seals for low pressure saturated steam but with the advent of superheating and higher pressure something more substantial was required. Several forms of metallic packing were developed and a number of different types are used for British locomotives. All employ segments of brass or cast iron and springs to provide a contact force. In some cases garter springs hold the segments firmly on the rod whilst in others coil and clip springs are used to provide contact between rod, segments and gland box. The type shown found extensive use in Britain.

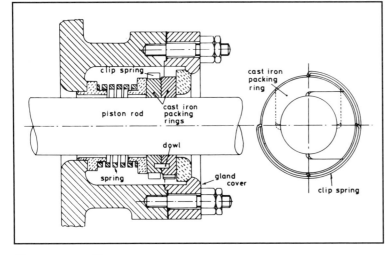

Above *LNER design 'A1' 'Pacific' No 60117,* Bois Roussel; *the superheater anti-vacuum valve may be seen just behind the chimney.* (D.K. Jones Collection)

Left *Metallic gland packing as used for many British super-heated locomotives.*

Compounding

To this point simple expansion of steam has been considered, that is steam expanded only in one cylinder before passing to exhaust. It is possible to expand steam to successively lower pressures in a number of stages with cylinders of increasingly larger size. In the late 19th and early 20th centuries a number of different compounding systems were developed for use in Britain but compounding never found as much favour there as it did elsewhere. Only the Midland railway persisted with compound locomotives, the arrangement employed being a development of the Smith system. One of these Midland compounds, No 1000, has been preserved. Compounding discussed here deals with general principles but relates to that class of locomotive in particular.

It is possible to make better use of high-pressure steam if it is expanded to low pressure but practical factors limit the degree of expansion which can be used in a single cylinder, simple engine, particularly the length of stroke required. If that expansion is divided between a number of cylinders, one after the other in series, complete expansion can be achieved with reasonable stroke and crank sizes. Other factors, including a reduction in the loss of energy due to condensation, make compounding theoretically advantageous. The reduction in loss caused by cylinder condensation occurs because the degree of expansion in

Cylinder arrangements for the Midland Compounds.

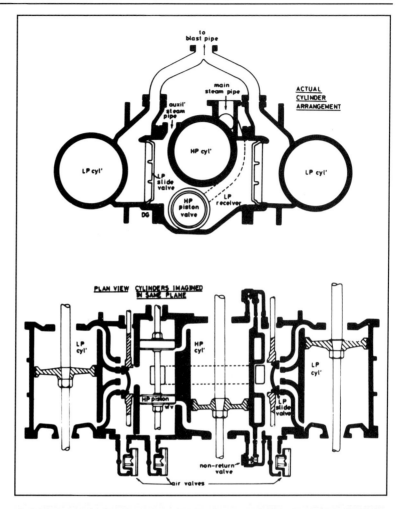

Midland Compound locomotive No 1000.

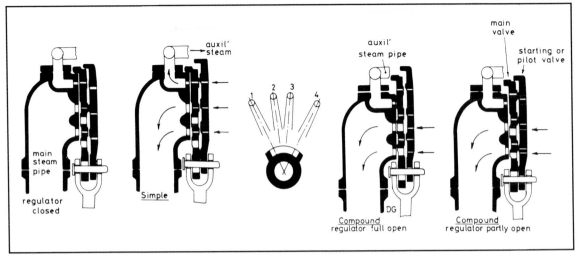

any cylinder is relatively small and so the corresponding fall in temperature is also reduced. Incoming steam at the next cycle does not meet cylinder walls which are too cold and so condensation is not likely to take place.

Practical considerations of compounding relate to the number and positioning of cylinders. The arrangement adopted by the Midland Railway had a single high-pressure (HP) cylinder between the frames and two low-pressure (LP) cylinders outside. All drove cranks on the leading coupled axle of these 4–4–0 locomotives, outside cranks being set at 90° to each other. The HP cylinder had a 482 mm (19 in) bore whilst that of the LP cylinders was 533 mm (21 in); all had 660 mm (26 in) strokes. To allow for positioning the HP cylinder centre was raised slightly relative to the LP cylinders. Slide valves directed steam and exhaust for the LP cylinders but a piston valve was provided for the HP.

During normal compound operation exhaust steam from the HP cylinder was directed to both LP cylinders, that exhaust entering an LP receiver between the frames with connection to both LP cylinders via their valves. Exhaust from the LP cylinders would pass to the blast pipe. Arrangements were such that locomotives could be operated as simples when starting and then changed to compound for normal running, higher power being required for start-

ing. This was achieved by means of the R.M. Deeley-designed regulator, a vertical unit with two valves, a main valve running on the valve face and a starting or pilot valve outside of that. Each valve was provided with a number of ports and could be moved to a particular position by means of a cranked arm operated by the regulator.

Movement of the regulator one-third of its travel (position 2) allowed both valves to direct full pressure steam to the LP receiver, via the auxiliary steam pipe, and also directed a small quantity of steam to the HP cylinder. Movement of the regulator full over (position 4) would shut off live steam to the LP receiver and direct steam only to the HP piston valve. The locomotive would then work as a compound with exhaust steam from the HP cylinder going to the LP receiver and hence to the LP cylinders. Pulling the regulator back slightly from the full open position to position 3 gave a reduced steam flow but still maintained compound working. With less steam consumption this position was used in conjunction with the cut-off adjustment.

When working as a simple with full pressure steam directed into the LP receiver it was possible for excess pressure to build up in the exhaust side of the HP piston with the piston valve providing connection between LP receiver and exhaust side of the piston. Such a situation could produce a negative turning moment on the HP crank which would reduce the turning force. To guard against such a situation non-return valves were placed at the ends of the HP cylinder. These would lift when receiver pressure exceeded pressure on the steam side of the HP piston and so equalize pressure on both sides of that piston. Compounding failed to make an impact in Britain but the preserved Midland Compound does allow a glimpse of what once was.

Valves and valve gear

Valves are employed to direct live steam to a

cylinder and exhaust steam away. Accurate control of these valves is essential for the locomotive to perform efficiently and the required power obtained. Apart from the correct timing of cylinder events, the opening and closing of admission and exhaust, port areas must be large so that steam can flow quickly to and from a cylinder. It is also ideal if valves can be made to cover and uncover ports as fast as possible so that full flow takes place in the limited time available.

Slide valves of 'D' form found use with non-superheated steam engines but they fell quickly from favour with the introduction of superheated steam (see page 48). Valve lead has

Above left *Deeley compound regulator.*

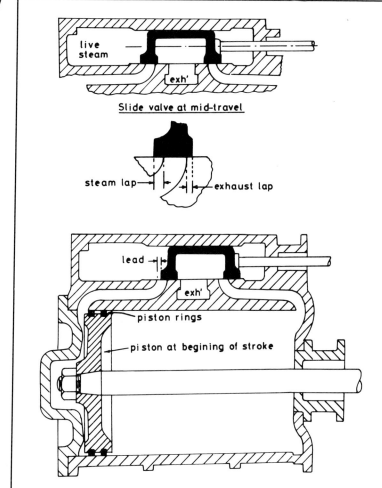

Right *'D' valve arrangement showing lap and lead.*

already been considered but valves are also provided with lap. This is the amount by which the valve covers the port on the steam and exhaust sides when the valve is in mid-position. Steam lap is the amount by which the port is covered on the steam side whilst exhaust lap is the covering of the same port on the exhaust side. Steam lap allows live steam supply to be shut off earlier in the stroke in order to provide expansive working without influencing the ability of the valve to provide other features such as lead. For most British locomotives sufficient lap is provided to allow a cut-off of 75 per cent when in full gear, i.e. when the reversing gear allows maximum valve travel. Exhaust, or inside, lap delays the point at which steam is released from the cylinder and so increases the amount of expansive working which might take place. Similarly it allows the exhaust to be covered earlier on the piston's next stroke thereby increasing the amount of compression. The amount of exhaust or inside lap must be considered carefully for particular types of locomotive, especially with regard to speed. At high operating speeds back pressure due to late release and compression can be excessive and so exhaust lap is usually only found on lower speed engines.

Valve travel is the distance a valve moves at full stroke and its amount governs both the speed at which ports are uncovered and the maximum size of port available. Large ports which are uncovered quickly allow steam, and exhaust, to flow with the minimum of obstruction, thus enabling maximum work to be produced. If full steam pressure can act on the piston right from commencement of the stroke maximum useful work will be obtained. Small valve areas provide a restriction which obstructs steam flow, especially at high piston speed, thus there is never a full steam pressure acting on the piston. It has already been mentioned that steam cannot flow instantaneously from one place to another and any constriction of the flow area not only slows down the flow but causes a slight pressure reduction. Long travel valves allow for large port openings which enables live and exhaust steam to flow with a minimum of delay or obstruction.

The setting of valves to give desired values of lap, lead and timing is a complex and highly skilled job which need not be discussed here. Type of valve gear as well as thermal expansion has to be taken into account and the reader can do no better than look at the description offered by D. W. Harvey in his fine volume, *A Manual of Steam Locomotive Preservation and Restoration.*

Slide valves have disadvantages. Not least amongst these is the amount of friction which occurs due to the rubbing between valve and steam chest. The energy required to operate such valves is considerable as high forces are needed to keep the valve on its seat in order to prevent leakage. Balanced type slide valves were developed to reduce this problem but the additional space they required made them unsuitable for most locomotives. The port area of slide valves is limited by the fact that the valve is rectangular and must be positioned alongside the curved cylinder, the port at each end of the cylinder only occupying the width of the valve. Slide valves invariably make use of outside steam which means that glands are subject to full live steam pressure.

Slide valve wear became a major problem with the introduction of superheated steam due to difficulties in satisfactorily lubricating the sliding faces because of the high temperatures. Piston valves quickly replaced slide valves when superheating became standard practice but slide valves retained one advantage. Should cylinder pressure become excessive due to trapped condensate a slide valve will rise off its seat and act like a relief valve.

Piston valves, as the name implies, are rather like pistons. Each valve comprises two piston units positioned on the valve rod at either end of the steam chest where the ports are situated. That in itself is advantageous as steam passageways to either end of the cylinder are direct and straight with large cross-sectional area so that as little resistance as possible is offered to the

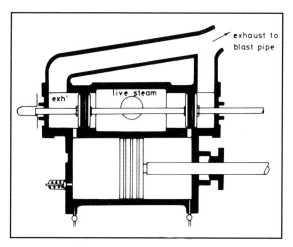

Cylinder arrangement for piston valves.

steam flow. As with cylinder pistons, rings are provided for sealing purposes. LMS pattern piston valves make use of up to six narrow piston rings whilst the GWR arrangement has a wide serrated ring which is forced into contact with the valve liner when under steam but falls back slightly when coasting, thus reducing wear.

Lap and lead can be provided as for slide valves but piston valves have no single face forced into contact with a seat, only weight forces the valve into contact with any part of its chest. Friction is less, lubrication becomes easier and inside steam may be used without problems because high steam pressure does not force the valve into contact with any face. Valves are balanced and the only friction is that which exists due to weight, the gland and the force of piston valve rings in contact with the steam chest. Tests have shown that the force required to operate a piston valve is less than 20 per cent of that needed to move a slide valve for similar duties.

A major advantage of the piston valve is that it provides for very large port areas. Valves actually run in liners fitted in the steam chests, liners being replaceable when wear makes it necessary. These liners, which are 'shrunk in', have ports extending around the full circumference. Width of ports is set to suit valve travel

and width of valve. A 254 mm (10 in) diameter piston valve has a circumference of 798 mm (31.41 in). Even allowing ports to occupy only 75 per cent of the circumference provides an equivalent slide valve port width of 599 mm (23.56 in). Placing a slide valve that wide above, below or alongside any cylinder would impose problems.

For operating valves many types of valve gear have been developed over the years but three main types predominate. Whatever the type of gear it is essential that valve timing is maintained accurately throughout the operating cycle. Valve gear for slide and piston valves may be a link motion or of the radial type. The difference relates to the manner in which motion is imparted to the valve. In the latter, valve movement comes from the combined effect of two eccentric motions whilst radial gear dispenses with eccentrics either partly or completely.

Stephenson gear is a link motion which found early acceptance for British locomotives although, contrary to its name, it was not a development of either George or Robert Stephenson, its design being credited to

Semi-plug piston valve as used by the GWR.

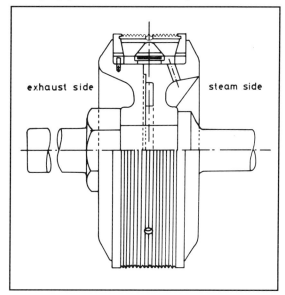

The top figure is a labelled line drawing with the following labels: reversing rod, reversing arm, crankshaft, eccentrics, suspension link, valve rod, fore gear link, back gear link, valve spindle, expansion link, piston rod, crosshead.

Above *Stephenson link motion as fitted to GWR locos.*

Left *Stephenson link motion: expansion link, suspension link, link arm connections and valve rod.*

William Howe, a pattern maker employed by the firm of Robert Stephenson and Co. Variations in construction exist depending upon whether the gear is inside or outside the frames. Inside operation has two eccentrics driven by the same crankshaft whilst outside gear makes use of two return cranks connected to a driving wheel. The actual mechanism is still the same, the difference lying in the means of imparting motion to the fore and back links attached to the expansion link.

The GWR made considerable use of inside Stephenson link motion with inside steam admission, the description and diagram shown relating to that arrangement. Eccentrics are positioned on the crankshaft such that the forward eccentric provides the correct amount of valve travel when operating at full power in the forward direction whilst the back eccentric does the same for going in reverse. The fore gear link connects with the upper part of the expansion link whilst the back gear link attaches at the bottom. That expansion link can be raised or lowered from the cab by means of the reversing rod and a system of levers. Within a slot in the expansion link runs a die block connected to a suspension link for support, and one end of the valve rod. That rod may connect directly to the valve spindle, via a pivoted support, or through a rocking shaft if the valve spindle is not in line with the valve rod. Such is the case for outside cylinder GWR locomotives which have inside valve gear.

With the expansion link positioned at its lowest point the die block is at the top of the link and the fore eccentric provides all of the operating motion. With the expansion link at its highest position the die block is at the bottom and the back eccentric provides correct valve motion for moving in reverse. With the expansion link positioned so that the die block is at the central position each eccentric provides the same amount of motion but with different timings which cancel out. In effect the expansion link rocks to and fro as if pivoting about its central point. The die block at that position imparts a motion to the valve equal in magnitude to the sum of laps and leads. This is mid gear where the locomotive is at rest or coasting and no steam is supplied to the cylinder.

Any movement of the expansion link up or down causes one of the eccentrics to have a greater influence on valve rod motion than the other thus giving a different amount of movement and timing to the valve. This allows the quantity of steam and the direction of operation to be changed if required. Stephenson link motion gives a change in valve lead with change in cut-off. The amount of lead is increased as the valve travel is reduced and is maximum when the die block is at centre of the expansion link.

Two different types of Stephenson link motion exist, locomotive type and launch type, the only difference being the points of connection at the expansion link for the rods from the eccentrics. In the locomotive type, used with slide valves, attachments are positioned further out than the extreme positions of the die blocks whilst with the launch type, used with piston valves, attachments are nearer to the middle of the expansion link. For the same size of eccentric the launch type allows longer valve travel—which is normally required with piston valves. In theory eccentrics must be positioned 90° ahead and behind the crank, the forward eccentric trailing by 90° and the backward eccentric leading by a similar amount. In practice the angles are reduced slightly in order to provide lead. This is known as the angle of advance because the forward eccentric gives advanced valve motion or lead. Thus if the angle of advance was 15° the forward eccentric would be 75° behind the crank and the backwards eccentric 75° ahead of it.

The arrangement described is that used by the GWR with its inside steam piston valves. Other systems employing Stephenson link motion differ slightly in terms of construction but the basic arrangement remains much the same. An LMS Class '5' locomotive No 4767, fortunately preserved, was fitted with outside Stephenson link motion using return cranks but this type of valve gear generally found use between the frames where space was available for eccentrics.

At this point it is worth mentioning the term 'notching up' which can cause confusion. It may be assumed that notching up means to increase the cut-off and engine power but the opposite is true. The expansion link for earlier engines was moved by means of a single reversing lever which operated through the reversing rod. With the lever in mid position the expansion link would also be in mid position and no steam would be supplied to the cylinders. For starting a steam locomotive maximum steam supply is required and so the control lever is moved to an extreme position giving maximum cut-off. As the locomotive builds up speed the control lever will be moved toward its mid point thereby reducing the cut-off and steam supply. This is notching up.

The control lever can be kept in a particular position by means of a spring-loaded pawl which engages with one of the notches in the plate at the foot of the lever. These notches prevent movement of the lever, and hence the expansion link, as the locomotive operates,

thus once set the degree of cut-off remains the same until the driver alters it. Because it was usual to have the control lever pulled right back for full gear, going ahead it would be pushed forward, notched up, in order to reduce the amount of cut-off. With screw reversers the same terminology remained although there were no longer any notches to consider. A screw reverser had to be made with threads on the screws of fine pitch so that creeping away from the set position did not take place. In order to avoid possible confusion I prefer to refer to cut-off rather than notching up.

Walschaerts gear is the most common radial type used in Britain both for inside and outside drives. Only one eccentric or crank, known as a return crank, is required to provide the valve motion and that makes it ideal for outside drives and saves space with inside drives. As with all radial gears the lead remains constant at all cut-offs. The single eccentric or crank connects with the bottom of the expansion link which is pivoted at its mid length. A link block, which is a sliding fit in the expansion link, is attached to a radius rod which has connections

Outside Stephenson link motion as fitted to preserved 'Black Five' No 44767.

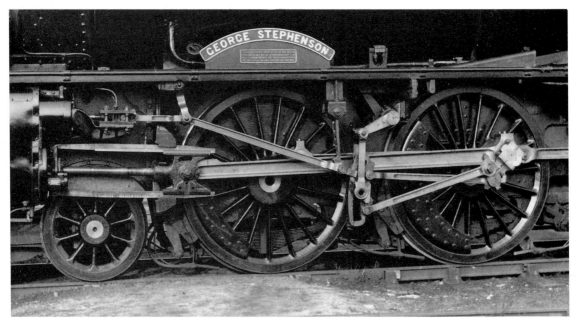

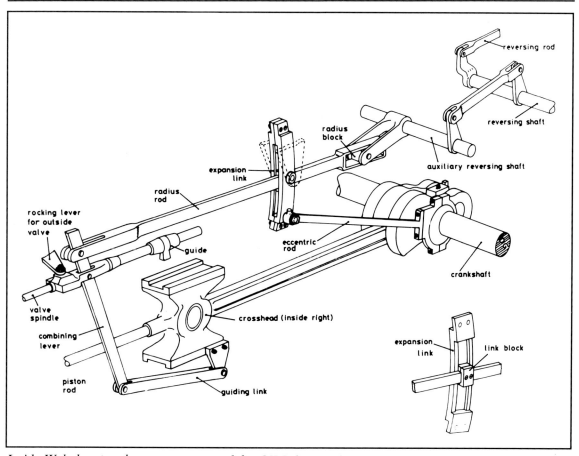

Inside Walschaerts valve gear as arranged for GWR locomotives.

with the reversing linkage. These connections are via a radius block at its rear end and a combining lever at the front end. The other end of the combining lever is given a motion from the crosshead by a guiding link. The valve spindle is actuated by the combining link thus valve movement is produced by the joint actions of crosshead and eccentric, or return crank.

The system is set so that the motion imparted to the valve by the eccentric or return crank is 90° ahead or behind that from the crosshead. Inside steam admission requires the eccentric or return crank to be behind the main crank whilst for outside admission it is ahead. Inside admission has the radius rod connecting with the combining lever above the valve spindle

whilst for outside admission the connection is below the valve spindle. Most locomotives employ inside steam admission with this form of gear but notable exceptions are the rebuilt Bulleid 'Pacifics'. This follows from the original Bulleid type of inside chain-driven gear which actuated outside admission steam valves by means of levers.

Reversing and alteration of cut-off with Walschaerts gear is achieved by raising or lowering the die block in its expansion link. This is done by means of the reversing rod which, through reversing shafts, raises or lowers the rear end of the radius rod. With the die block at the middle of the expansion link there is no contribution to valve motion from the eccentric: maximum contribution occurs

Above *Outside Walschaerts gear as fitted to LMS '8F'.*   **Below** *Joy valve gear.*

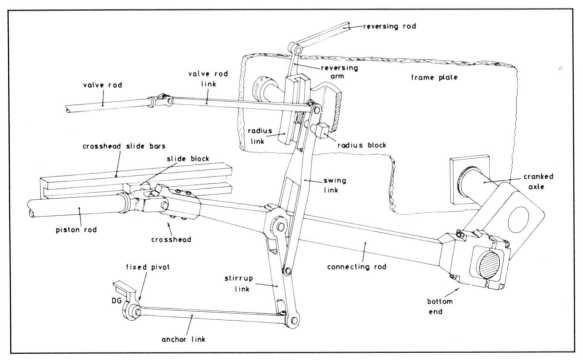

when the die block is at either extreme end of the expansion link. Lead depends upon the stroke of the crosshead and is set by the relative lengths of the connecting levers, rods and links. Careful design, construction and assembly of these is necessary to ensure optimum timing of valve events. Walschaerts gear can be seen in action amongst the ranks of preserved locomotives, the main variation being that of the rebuilt Bulleid Pacifics already mentioned.

Another radial type of valve gear for consideration is that introduced by David Joy in 1879 and known by his name. Joy valve gear requires no eccentrics or return cranks, motion being taken from the connecting rod. This fact made it very suitable for inside cylinders and that is where it found most application, although a few outside cylinder examples were produced. Drilling of the connecting rod for attachment of the stirrup or correcting link, was considered by some to be a bad practice which would weaken that part but no failures could ever be attributed solely to it. The stirrup link connects with an anchor link at its lower end, the anchor link attaching to a fixed pivot at its other end. Near the central point of the stirrup link is connected the lower end of a swing link, the upper end of which is attached to the valve rod. Just below that point are fitted the pivoting radius blocks which slide in the curved channels of the radius link. This link is pivoted at its central point and can be made to tilt by means of the reversing rod.

Again careful design and construction of links was necessary in order to produce the correct valve timings and provide the desired lead. As the connecting rod swings when the locomotive is running various linkages are set in motion especially the swing link. As this moves it causes the radius blocks to move up and down in the radius link and this, in combination with the fore and back movement of the swing link due to its lower end connection, brings about valve rod movement. When die blocks are at the centre of the radius link the valve will have minimum horizontal movement equal to twice the lap plus lead. This is set by the relative lengths of linkages and positions of pivot points.

Tilting of the radius link increases the amount of horizontal movement imparted to the valve, the direction of tilt producing forward or backward gear. With outside steam where slide valves are used the top end of the radius link is tilted towards the cylinder for forwards operations whilst for running in reverse it is tilted away from the cylinder.

Joy gear found considerable use with Lancashire & Yorkshire Railway locomotives and those of the LNWR and a number of examples from these railways have been preserved. Unfortunately these locomotives are fitted with inside gear which does not make for easy observation. Joy gear fell from favour as outside cylinders became popular because of the difficulty in providing for an anchor link attachment to the main frames. Alternatives to that link make the arrangement complex and inferior to Walschaerts gear in terms of steam distribution.

The systems described so far have concerned arrangements for single cylinders but it is possible to make one set of gear operate valves for two cylinders on a four-cylinder locomotive. GWR 'Castle' and 'King' designs had the valves for outside cylinders driven through rocking levers by the same gear which operated the inside cylinders on the other side of the frame. For LMS 'Duchess' Class locomotives the opposite was true in that one set of outside Walschaerts gear operated outside and inside cylinder valves on that side of the locomotive, again rocking levers imparting the motion. Such arrangements were only possible because respective outside and inside cylinder pairs had their cranks at 180° to each other. When one piston moved forward the other moved backwards and the valves had similar relative motions: simple rocking levers sufficed. In the case of the GWR locos those levers were cranked slightly in order to account for connecting rod angularity not corrected due to use of horizontal cylinders.

A more complicated system is required for a three-cylinder locomotive but valves for the inside cylinder may be actuated by the combined motions of the two outside cylinder valve rods acting through a conjugated lever. This system was popular on the LNER but found little use elsewhere.

Any valve gear has to provide unobstructed flow paths for live and exhaust steam in order that the highest possible powers might be achieved. Slide and piston valves, no matter

Left *'Castle' Class outside cylinder and valve chest showing rocking lever for operating valve from inside gear.*

Left *'Black Five' No. 44757 fitted with Caprotti valves – the operating shaft for the valve gear was between the locomotive frames.* (D.K. Jones collection)

Left *Caprotti valve chest, drive and reversing shafts of the preserved BR Class '8' 'Pacific',* Duke of Gloucester.

Right *Arrangement of cylinder and valve chest for the* Duke of Gloucester.

how well designed, do impose restrictions to some extent and poppet valve systems were developed in an attempt to overcome them. As with many things the theory proved to be more effective than the practice and no arrangement showed itself to be any advance upon a well-found piston valve installation. British-Caprotti valve gear turned out to be more effective than the rest but the demise of steam on British railways limited its application. Fitting of Caprotti gear to a number of 'Black 5s' and a few standard class locomotives showed what might have been achieved but the main application was to the unique three-cylinder Class '8' standard locomotive No 71000, *Duke*

of Gloucester. As No 71000 has been preserved the following description relates to that installation.

Double beat poppet valves allow maximum area for steam flow with a timing that is extremely accurate, thus offering the full potential of a poppet valve system. Each of the three cylinders is provided with its own valve housing incorporating two inlet and two exhaust valves, a pair for each side of the piston. Rotating cams provide the opening force for each valve, rotation coming from shafts driven by the central coupled wheels through a bevel gear box. Drive for the centre cylinder cam box comes from the left side drive shaft. Apart

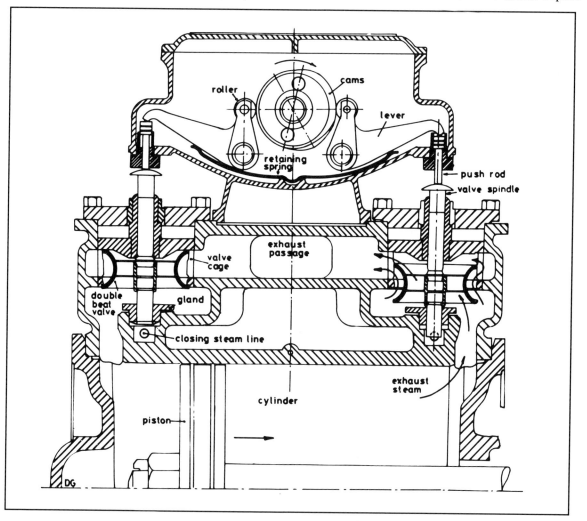

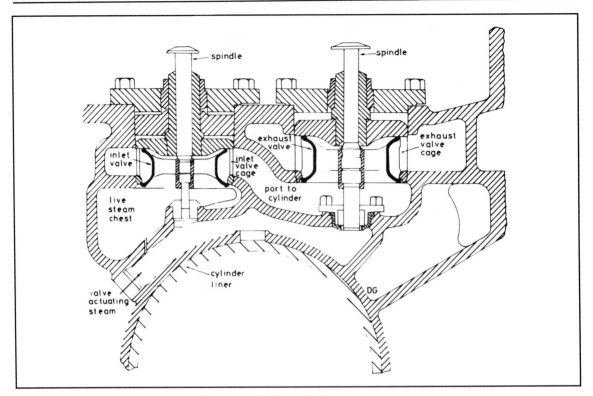

Caprotti inlet and exhaust valves for one end of a cylinder.

from the drives each of the three cam boxes is essentially the same and so only one needs to be considered.

Each inlet and exhaust valve, connected to a spindle, is opened by means of a push rod which is actuated by a cam-operated lever. Although the cam roller levers are spring-loaded in order to keep rollers in contact with their respective cams the valves are not spring-loaded. The closing force for each valve is obtained from steam acting on the lower face of its spindle. This avoids the use of springs with their associated problem of breakage and also allows the valves to drop open when main steam is shut off during periods of coasting. Both inlet and exhaust valves operate in a very similar way although the cam lever systems differ in detail rather than principle. When a cam acts against a roller the lever moves and forces open its valve in just the same way as valves on a car or motorcycle engine operate.

Unlike the car engine, however, it is necessary to arrange for the steam locomotive valve gear to vary the period of steam admission and to reverse rotational direction.

A very clever system of moving cams provides for change in steam admission and reversing: only steam cams will be described as their operation is more critical than that of the exhaust cams. Control of exhaust valves is completely separate from the inlet valves and so it is possible to maintain release and compression periods to suit any degree of cut-off.

Each valve lever has two rollers which run on two cams placed alongside each other. These cams are capable of relative rotational movement whilst still being turned by the drive shaft. If the cams are rotated away from each other the period during which the rollers are lifted, and hence the valve is open, is increased. With the cams rotated towards each other so that they overlap forming the smallest cam when viewed along the shaft, the period of opening is a minimum and equal to the angular size of that arrangement. Each cam is provided with a pair of rods for bringing about movement and these rods may be rotated relative to the drive shaft by means of a collar. The collar sits on a screwed thread which forms part of the rotating drive shaft but can be moved axially along that screw thread by means of sleeve bearing. Sleeves remain still but the collars rotate with the drive shaft. Movement of the sleeves is by means of arms from the reversing shaft. By this means both cam portions may be repositioned whilst they rotate and so alter the timing for inlet valve opening and closing.

It is not really necessary to understand how the cams are repositioned in order to appreciate the valve gear. It is sufficient just to understand that moving the two cam portions on the camshaft allows the cut-off to be changed and the timing altered for reversal. Greater angular spacing between the cam portions means a larger degree of cut-off and more steam going to the cylinder.

When working as designed Caprotti gear was as effective as any ever devised but the railways of Britain were not really equipped for maintaining and overhauling it. Little expertise developed and it was never really allowed to show its full potential. As far as the footplate crew was concerned there was no difference in cab controls but the enthusiast noticed a difference in the absence of flashing valve levers. *Duke of Gloucester* has drive shafts on either side but 'Black 5s' had shafts between the frames.

Crossheads and slide bars

A crosshead simply translates reciprocating motion of the piston rod into semi-rotary motion at that end of the connecting rod. A bearing is, therefore, essential and crosshead must be provided for each piston. Because of the angular position a connecting rod takes when rotating the driving wheels a vertical thrust is exerted at the crosshead, its magnitude and direction depending upon piston force,

Steam inlet valve cam box.

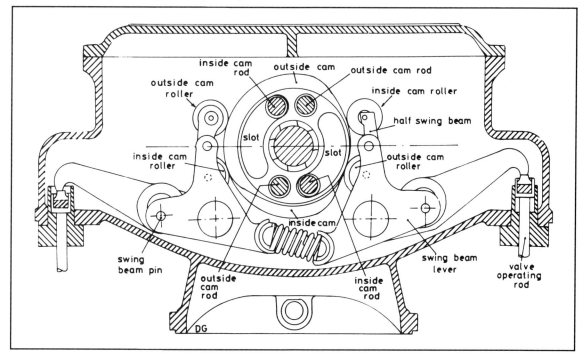

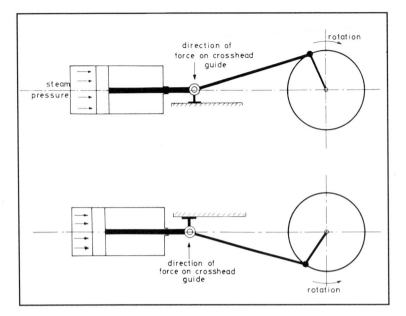
steam pressure

direction of
force on crosshead
guide

rotation

direction of
force on crosshead
guide

rotation

Left *Diagram showing direction of forces on crosshead guide bars.*

Right *Bulleid design of crosshead and slide bars.*

angular position of the connecting rod and rotational direction of the wheel.

Consider first the diagram with steam forcing the piston downwards and the wheel rotating in a clockwise direction (reverse as far as a locomotive would be concerned). With the crank above the axle to crosshead centreline it will be understood that the compressive force in the connecting rod will exert a force in a downwards direction at the crosshead because an upwards force is exerted at the crank in order to produce rotation. This downwards force must be balanced hence the fitting of slide bars upon which the guide shoe may run. Steam on the other side of the piston pushes it back up the cylinder the force produced being such that it causes the connecting rod to pull the crank around. Because of this there is a tensile stress in the connecting rod which results in a downward pull on the crosshead. The same guide shoe takes the downward force.

If the locomotive is operated so that the wheel turns in an anti-clockwise direction (ahead drive) then similar reasoning indicates that the crosshead thrust acts upwards and a different slide bar is required. For locomotives which are required to reverse, and they all are, two faces of thrust must be provided by slide

bars. Different patterns are available to suit the ideas of different designers but they all perform the same basic task, namely to take vertical thrust due to the connecting rod's angular position and so avoid the piston being forced against the cylinder wall or the rod against the gland. That would result in excessive cylinder wear and gland damage which would cause steam leakage because the steam engine is double-acting. Bending of the piston rod could also take place.

Slide bars must be of the correct size for a particular engine in order to minimize loading. The area of contact should be high enough to reduce the risk of oil film breakdown which would cause high wear. Regular supply of lubricant to the slide bars is essential in order to avoid such wear and maintain the piston and its rod in correct alignment. For the same reason accurate setting of the slide bars with a new or overhauled locomotive is as essential as alignment of cylinders and axles.

Balancing

A factor ignored by many locomotive enthusiasts is that of balancing, probably because understanding of the principles involves a good

knowledge of mathematics. Appreciation of the difficulties involved in achieving effective balance, however, need not consider mathematics in detail although some must be used to show what forces exist. The enthusiast without leanings towards trigonometry or algebra may ignore these and just consider the forces involved. A steam locomotive requires balancing of reciprocating and rotating masses and if that is not confusing enough, some of the moving parts may be considered as producing *both* reciprocating and rotating forces!

Rotating masses basically concern the wheels and axles although parts of the coupling and connecting rods may also be considered as rotary. A perfectly-formed disc which is the same at all parts and without any added parts may be considered to be perfectly balanced as each portion of it exerts the same amount of centrifugal force. The idea of centrifugal force may be obtained by swinging around a weight on a piece of string, the string remains tight because of the centrifugal force exerted by the weight as it rotates. (This is a simplified explanation but we are trying to avoid technicalities.)

If a weight is added to the disc at any point around its rim, or nearer the centre for that matter, the disc will become unbalanced because of the centrifugal force exerted by that weight. That force will pull the disc to one side placing increased load on the bearing of the disc, the load being always at the side upon which the weight has been placed. The effect of unbalance may be observed with a spin dryer which has not been loaded evenly with wet clothes. If the disc, or a wheel, rotates with its axis horizontal, the out of balance force at times acts upwards and then downwards. This effect may be observed with car wheels which are out of balance. To correct that defect balance weights, small pieces of lead, are added to the rim of the wheel. The size and placing of such weights is carefully chosen so that they perfectly oppose all other centrifugal forces acting on the wheel. These forces may be due to design of the wheel or necessary parts like the air valve which are out of symmetry.

Adding such weights to a locomotive wheel allows perfect rotating balance to be achieved for items such as cranks, crank pins, webs, eccentrics, etc. Attempting to balance reciprocating masses, however, leads to additional forces.

The reciprocating masses are the piston, piston rod, crosshead and a portion of the connecting rod. Other masses are also present but they complicate any basic description even further. The most difficult situation exists with a two-cylinder locomotive and that is what will be considered. Movement of pistons down their cylinders produces a horizontal force that can cause a swaying motion the moment of which will depend upon several factors, including how far apart the cylinders are placed. The faster a piston moves, the higher will be the force exerted. A sideways motion can be unpleasant and even dangerous leading to derailment if excessive. Unbalanced reciprocating forces also cause a fore and aft motion of the locomotive.

By placing another piston in line with the first but acting in the opposite direction such reciprocating forces become balanced. Opposed-piston internal combustion engines achieve this balance in the same cylinder, examples of these being the Doxford marine engine and the Deltic engine. With steam locomotives having only two cylinders there is no possibility of such balancing but in a four-cylinder loco with inside and outside cylinders at each frame there is this possibility. Placing their cranks at 180° to each other allows one piston to be moving forwards and the other backwards thus allowing horizontal forces to cancel each other out.

For two-cylinder locomotives reciprocating masses have to be balanced by other masses moving in the opposite direction and that can only be done by placing masses on the driving wheels opposite to the crank and as far out as possible towards the wheel rim. As the reciprocating mass, M_r, moves down the cylinder the balance mass, M_b, moves in the other direction to cancel it out. If that was all there was to it then balancing would be easy but mechanics doesn't work that way! In order to obtain the opposing horizontal force from the balance weight it is positioned on the most appropriate driving mechanism, which happens to be a wheel. This actually rotates the balance weight, causing it to exert a centrifugal force which can be resolved into vertical and horizontal components. The horizontal component may be used

for balancing of horizontal reciprocating masses but what of the vertical component? It is that which causes the problem. The maximum vertical component of centrifugal force exists when the balance mass is directly above or below the axle. When above the force is upwards tending to lift the wheel from the track: when below that component is downwards causing a higher force to be exerted on the track over and above that due to static axle loading. This is a hammer blow which goes from zero with the crank at either end of the stroke to a maximum when the balance weight is at its lowest position: hammer blow is negative when the balance weight is at its highest position, as the force acts upwards.

From the above it can be seen that adding weights in order to reduce the swaying effect due to reciprocating masses serves to increase loading on the track in a most damaging fashion as hammer blow occurs. The magnitude of hammer blow depends upon the size of balance mass added, its distance from the centre of rotation and the speed of wheel rotation. Magnitude actually depends upon the square of the rotating speed, so the faster the wheels turn the greater will be the hammer blow, express trains being most susceptible because they have large diameter wheels which rotate at high speed. In true compromise tradition hammer blow is minimized by only balancing a portion of the reciprocating masses (usually two-thirds with a two-cylinder locomotive). This still allows some swaying but keeps hammer blow within reasonable limits. In the past locomotives were kept from certain routes because of bridge loading restrictions, hammer blow added to static axle loading having to be below a value set by the civil engineer. Speed reductions over bridges had to be observed in other cases in order to restrict hammer blow.

Hammer blow can be reduced by distributing the reciprocating balance mass over all of the coupled wheels rather than concentrating it just at the cranked wheel. Reciprocating masses remain partially balanced as before but centrifugal force induced by the balance mass is less. There is a centrifugal force, and hence a hammer blow, at each wheel but it is less than that which would exist if the entire mass was concentrated at a single wheel. Weights required to balance rotating masses must, however, be retained within the wheel to which they refer.

With four-cylinder locomotives, as already discussed, there is no requirement for large weights to balance reciprocating masses. The same is almost true for correctly designed three-cylinder locomotives with cranks positioned such that the net forward reciprocating force equates to the net backward reciprocating force. Designers might decide that slightly imperfect reciprocating balance could be tolerated and not use balance weights, thus avoiding the problem of hammer blow. It was all a matter of design and, to some extent, personal

preference with three and four-cylinder locomotives. Low masses for reciprocating parts such as pistons, rods, valve gear, etc. reduced the requirement for large reciprocating balance masses. Three-cylinder Bulleid 'Pacifics' had no reciprocating balance weights provided, light weight parts, the absence of outside valve gear, mainly rotating drive for the inside valve gear and good design all helped to reduce the need.

Balancing weights may be cast as part of the wheel if their magnitude is accurately known and if the designer is confident that the wheel centre will always require such a balance weight. Such would not be the case if the same sized wheel was to be employed for locomotives having different numbers of cylinders or coupled wheels. As reciprocating balance weights may be distributed amongst all coupled wheels less weight is applied to each wheel with four-coupled axles compared with only three. As rotary balancing weights may also be re-

Diagram of forces produced by balance weights.

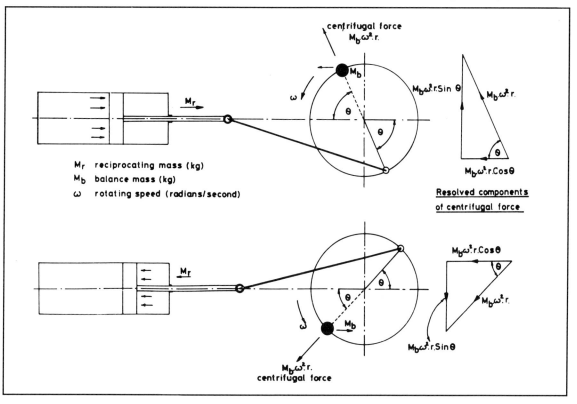

quired the actual total weight applied to each wheel will generally differ.

A common means of providing balancing weights was to rivet segments of plate near the rim of a wheel centre, inside and outside of the spokes. A measured quantity of molten lead would then be poured into the cavity formed and allowed to solidify. This method allowed any size of balance weight to be conveniently applied, and adjusted if necessary.

A further form of loading is imposed upon the driven wheels because of the action of the piston and connecting rod. With the connecting rod angled downwards a loading is applied to the wheel in the downward direction whilst when the crank is above the axle the force is upwards. These are static loads and are independent of speed but do depend upon the steam force applied to the piston. Maximum vertical loading exists at some point down the piston stroke, the actual position of the piston when that occurs being governed by the length of crank and length of connecting rod. At late cut-offs steam pressure remains high for some distance down the piston stroke and so the vertical force applied, up and down, will be at a maximum. As late cut-offs occur at starting when the locomotive is running slowly the downward force is not likely to add appreciably to total axle loading because hammer blow will be small at such speeds. The vertical forces imposed at the cranked wheels are basically opposite to the vertical forces at the crossheads.

Static axle loading is that due to the weight of a locomotive together with water in the boiler and fire in the grate, plus the weight of footplate crew. For tank engines water in the tank and coal in the bunker must also be considered. Weight distribution governs the loading on individual axles as does the spring adjustment. Springs transmit locomotive load to the axle boxes, control the rise and fall of those boxes and dampen out track shocks. If they are incorrectly set an axle might not take its designed load and that can result in problems of increased bearing wear and unpleasant riding. In Britain track condition has, in general, been good but overseas that would not necessarily be the case. In order to account for this compensated springing was used. Basically this consisted of a number of axles connected to the same set of springs by means of levers to spread any track imperfection over more axles.

Laminated springs are the most commonly used type, the central part connecting with the axle box and the two outer parts with the main frame. As with balancing, the design theory is rather involved mathematically and need not be discussed. The important thing is that upon initial set-up or after replacement wheel loading must be checked. Weighing equipment is available allowing the load on each wheel to be measured and any adjustment, at the spring hangers, made to give the correct wheel loadings.

The action of cylinders makes the wheels turn but there is more to a locomotive than simply getting it to move.

CHAPTER 4

Ancillary equipment

The boiler and engine systems of a steam locomotive may be its most obvious parts and those to which popular attention is given but they are far from being all that a locomotive is. Additional items are required to make for safer and more efficient operation as well as providing for improved convenience and extended running. As with the main systems several different arrangements were available for use with steam locomotives and there is no point trying to describe them all but I hope to explain their working by reference to typical examples.

Brakes

When giving evidence before the Gauge Commission Brunel was asked about the effectiveness of brakes fitted to GWR locomotives. His answer, 'Tolerably useless', typified the braking capacity of all locomotives of the period. Fortunately things improved!

Initially only locomotives and tenders were provided with any form of braking and this situation remained in force as far as freight working was concerned with the locomotive's steam or air brakes being the only means available for bringing both locomotive and train to rest. Continuous vacuum braking became standard for most railways with regards to passenger stock towards the latter part of the 19th century and, with but little modification, remained with British steam haulage until it ceased normal operations. A number of different vacuum arrangements were developed and put into use over the years. Basic operation of continuous vacuum brakes only will be considered, specific cases being left for the reader to discover. Before going into the vacuum system however it is opportune to deal with steam (or air) brakes.

In any brake system a cylinder with a moving piston is employed to actuate linkages which force brake shoes into contact with the wheel tyres. The piston in that cylinder may be forced to move by air or steam pressure but it really doesn't matter to the linkage what medium causes the movement, so long as there is one. Because steam brakes were only applied to locomotives and tenders their arrangement was fairly basic consisting of a cylinder containing a neat-fitting piston with rings, similar to the engine piston. Piston rod connected with the brake pull rod by means of a bell-crank lever which was spring-loaded. Whenever the steam brake valve was operated steam would flow to the top of the piston forcing it downwards and applying the brake. At the same time the spring would be compressed. For brake release the steam line would be vented allowing the return spring to move the piston back to the top of its cylinder and pull the brakes off.

In general terms all steam brakes operated in this fashion, and still do so on preserved steam locomotives. Differences lay in the way steam was applied to the cylinder as many locomotives would also be fitted with a vacuum brake system for working passenger trains or fitted freights. A combined steam and vacuum brake valve was provided by many designers, steam admission to the brake cylinder being controlled by the degree of vacuum in the train brake pipe. When that vacuum is destroyed steam is allowed to the steam brake cylinder via the combined valve, thus avoiding the need for the driver to concern himself with actuation of two sets of brakes, vacuum and steam. The combined valve does not simply allow steam to flow when air flows, but controls the rate at which steam flows after the vacuum has been partially destroyed. This ensures that train brakes are applied before locomotive steam brake thus avoiding a pushing effect from coaches or wagons on the locomotive. For a long train it takes time for brakes to be completely applied. With the brake valve handle moved to the 'brake off' position a vacuum is created in the train pipe and that allows a piston in the brake valve to move thus shutting off steam to the brake cylinder. This vents the cylinder and the steam brake is pulled off. Operation of the steam brake is, therefore, essentially the same as the vacuum brake to be described below, only the operating medium differs.

Vacuum brakes work because air pressure on one side of a piston is allowed to force that piston upwards and so apply brakes through a system of levers. With the brakes off a train pipe which connects with the lower face of the piston is maintained under vacuum, the upper face of the piston is kept under vacuum at all times. Weight keeps the piston in its lowest position and so the brakes are not applied. With air allowed into the train pipe the piston is forced upwards and applies the brake. Over the years several variations have been tried and a number of modifications made but the basic principle has remained the same. Brake cylinders differ slightly through the use of alternative arrangements for sealing and different types of internal valves as well as by provision of integral air reservoirs in certain cases. Brake cylinders are generally designated by letters

such as type 'C', type 'E' and type 'F', each having slightly different features which it is unnecessary to discuss in detail: the actual type of vacuum cylinder employed for a practical installation depends upon the brake system itself but in most cases they are interchangeable between systems. The cylinder diagram illustrates the principle rather than a particular type.

A piston, the rod of which connects with the brake linkage, is a fairly neat fit in its cylinder. Near the top of the piston on its outer face is a groove, the relieving groove, which holds a rubber ring when at the lower part of the cylinder. As the piston moves upwards during operation the rubber ring rolls out of its groove and rolls upwards between piston and cylinder thus maintaining a good seal with the minimum of friction. It is essential that all moving parts on a brake cylinder move with the least frictional resistance in order to ensure that maximum force is available for braking. The hole at the bottom of the piston rod is actually elongated slightly in order to allow the piston to move by a small amount to get the ring out of its groove before any load from the linkage is applied.

Upward movement of the piston is brought about by air pressure from below, induced by the destruction of the train pipe vacuum due to application of the brake valve. For the cylinder shown, although not for all types of cylinder, there is a vacuum reservoir surrounding the top portion which is maintained under vacuum condition during brake application. Vacuum is never absolute, there always being some air at very much reduced pressure present. Vacuum is usually measured as a column of mercury, normal atmospheric air pressure of 1 bar (14.5 psi) being capable of supporting 762 mm (30 in) of mercury. A vacuum of 533 mm (21 in) actually means that the pressure has been reduced by an amount equal to a 533 mm (21 in) column of mercury. It does not mean that the train brake pipe pressure could support a column of mercury that tall. In effect the pressure is much lower than the figures seem to

Vacuum brake cylinder.

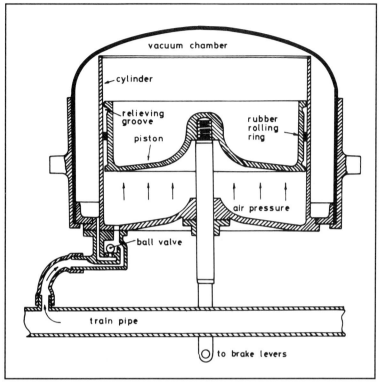

indicate. The term 'a vacuum of' implies that the pressure has been reduced by that amount, thus 'a vacuum of 533 mm (21in)' actually means that the pressure in the train pipe could support 762 mm − 533 mm = 229 mm of mercury. In absolute terms the pressure in the train pipe is about 0.3 bar (4.35 psi). Perfect vacuums are almost impossible to obtain and unnecessary in this situation anyway.

When the brake is applied the piston moves upwards and low pressure air above the piston is compressed thus increasing its pressure. This higher pressure acting downwards against the upward movement of the piston could reduce the force of the brake application. To avoid such impediment to brake effectiveness, especially if any air leaks past the sealing ring, vacuum reservoirs are often fitted. These large volume chambers maintain a reserve of vacuum which enables high brake forces to be produced even when the brake cylinder piston movement is large due to wear of brake shoes. In certain cases, for locomotives and tenders,

plain cylinders without reservoirs are used but a vacuum reservoir will then be incorporated in the brake line.

In most vacuum brake installations the driver's brake valve is combined with the ejectors which form and maintain vacuum in the train pipe. Where applicable a mechanism for operating the steam brake would also be incorporated. Visually the valve is very easy to see in a cab for it is fitted with a brass disc or cylinder on the body, this containing many small holes through which air can flow. Movement of the control lever on this valve to the braking position allows air into the train pipe thus destroying the vacuum. Under normal braking conditions gentle application is required in order to avoid jerking of the train, the vacuum being destroyed gradually but not completely.

Experience of the line and an understanding of the train is required by the driver in order to allow him to assess the optimum braking requirements for bringing the train to a stand at the desired position. Late and sudden braking can result in jerking which could cause passenger injury. A small reduction in train pipe vacuum is sufficient to allow gentle application of the brake which allows for stopping at the required position. As soon as the train is at rest the ejector may be used to restore vacuum and so release the brakes ready for restarting.

In the guard's compartment at the end of the train there is a hand-controlled brake valve which the guard may use should he desire to brake the train for any reason. This valve is also capable of opening automatically should the driver apply his brake in a hard manner in order to bring the train to rest quickly. If the train pipe vacuum falls below a predetermined value, indicating a sudden, quick application of the brake, the guard's valve will open and allow air into that end of the train pipe thereby allowing for faster application of the brakes along the coaches and wagons connected by flexible brake (vacuum) pipes. Should the train part, one of these pipes will fail and allow air into both sections of the train thus alerting both driver and guard and applying the brakes in both sections.

For all recent vacuum brake systems, including those of preserved railways, the approved method of passengers wishing to attract the attention of driver and guard in an emergency is through the train brake pipe. The communication cord, actually a chain, in each compartment is attached to a lever which can operate a flap valve. The flap valve covers the end of a branch pipe which connects with the train pipe. When the chain is pulled for whatever reason the lever acts to lift the flap valve and allow air into the train pipe. The pipe, about 16 mm diameter, does not allow sufficient air flow to completely destroy the vacuum and so bring the train to rest but it allows some application which indicates to the driver that something is wrong. The driver may then stop the train in a convenient position. The communication cord is a means of summoning assistance and not necessarily for the urgent application of the brakes by a passenger: only the driver or guard should ever be in a position to bring a train to rest since full application of the brake by means of the communication cord might mean stopping in a tunnel or some other dangerous position which could increase the hazard for passengers and footplate crew alike. The guard may discover in which compartment the alarm has been actuated by inspection of the loose chain and raised flap valve. To resume normal

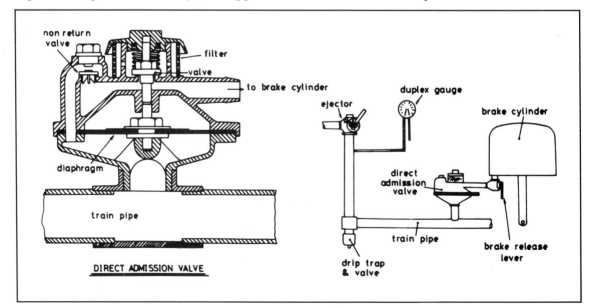

DIRECT ADMISSION VALVE

operation the valve is simply rotated so that it again covers the end of the branch pipe and seals it.

For long trains, passenger or freight, fast application of brakes cannot be ensured simply by means of the driver's brake valve even with the assistance of that in the guard's compartment and direct admission valves were devised for this purpose. Fitted in the line which connects each cylinder to the train pipes, these devices allow air to act on the piston directly from atmosphere rather than the train pipe. Although the actual pattern of construction may differ the basic principle is that increase in train pipe pressure due to brake applications, causes a diaphragm to lift and that in turn opens a valve which allows air from the atmosphere to act on the piston. With such valves the train pipe vacuum has only to be marginally destroyed and each brake cylinder will then be able to apply its brake by the same amount irrespective of its position in the train. The degree of brake application still depends upon the amount of vacuum destruction in the train pipe and thus the driver can still control brake application.

Following brake application with air pressure below the piston and vacuum above, it may be necessary to release one or more brakes quickly, say for detachment of a coach with brakes kept on the others. Hand release of brakes is accomplished by allowing air into the space above the piston: with pressures equalized above and below, the piston will fall due to gravity and so release the brake. A valve, usually operated by a chain acting through a lever, may be opened to provide access for the air to reach the space above the piston. Different cylinders have different arrangements and the valve may be a completely separate unit or may simply consist of a mechanism for displacing the ball valve as shown in the brake cylinder diagram. With this non-return ball valve off its seat air from the train pipe can pass through a small hole normally covered by the ball valve and find its way to the piston top.

With a vacuum brake system it is essential that a device be provided to remove any air which leaks into the train pipe. This device must also be capable of evacuating air from the pipe in order to release the brakes following an application. Vacuum pumps, as used by the GWR and described later, will perform that duty when the locomotive is running but the steam-operated air ejector found more general application.

Left *Direct admission valve.*

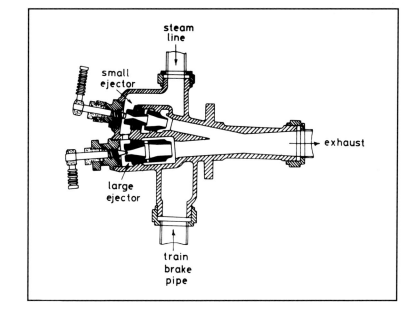

Right *Combined air ejector.*

Most ejectors comprise two separate units within the same casing: a large ejector to create a new vacuum in the train brake pipe following brake application and a small ejector to maintain the vacuum during continuous running. Both operate in the same way but the larger unit is capable of removing air from the brake pipe at a higher rate: it also uses much more steam and so is not economical for continuous running, hence the small ejector. Large and small ejectors are connected to the same brake pipe and exhaust into the same pipe which discharges up the locomotive chimney.

The only difference between the large and small ejectors is in the size of nozzle and so it is only necessary to describe the action in general terms. The driver operates a handwheel or lever control to open a valve which admits steam into the nozzle inlet. This convergent-divergent nozzle has the effect of increasing the steam's velocity to a very high level at its exit (see Appendix). The high speed jet of steam draws air with it (due to the effect of friction) and the air/steam mixture passes through the converging nozzle into the outlet side of the ejector casing. The suction side of the casing is connected to the train brake pipe and results in a vacuum forming, or being maintained, in that pipe. Double non-return valves at the inlet to each ejector prevent air or steam from flowing back into the train pipe and thus

destroying the vacuum.

Steam-operated ejectors are certainly effective but they can consume a considerable quantity of steam especially if any air is leaking into the system. Ejectors also suffer from the disadvantage that if steam production is poor (due to low-quality coal, clinker build-up or other conditions for example) the brakes will gradually creep on as steam pressure falls. With the locomotive already struggling due to poor steaming the extra effort required to overcome brakes can result in the train drawing to a stop. Only fire cleaning and raising the steam pressure will then get things moving again! A number of railways utilized vacuum pumps rather than small ejectors for constant use though large ejectors were still being fitted for use when the locomotive was at rest.

The Great Western was the most common user of vacuum pumps and the double-acting pumps fitted to GWR locomotives differed little from the introduction of the device in the late 19th century until that company's design of locomotives ceased to be manufactured. Driven by a connection from one of the crossheads the pump worked whenever the wheels turned and maintained the GWR brake vacuum of 635 mm (25 in) of mercury. This was higher than most other railway companies and caused no problems when every part of the train was designed for it, but through working of GWR

stock which required an engine change did result in some inconvenience. With such a high vacuum it was necessary to release all coaching stock brakes and then remake the vacuum following attachment of the other locomotive which invariably maintained a standard 533 mm (21 in) vacuum.

Double-acting pumps remained relatively free from defects and highly efficient in terms of vacuum production: in many respects too efficient. Too high a vacuum when running creates a low pressure above the brake piston which can result in an inability to release the brake after it has been used if the ejecter proves unable to lower train pipe pressure to that formed when the locomotive was running. A similar situation could result with steam-operated large and small ejectors but is less likely for the more usual 533 mm brake vacuum. In order to prevent high vacuum formation with pump and ejector systems relief valves are provided. These allowed air into the train pipe if the pressure falls below that normally required, i.e. if the vacuum becomes too great.

With any low pressure system water vapour can be a problem and thus the removal of condensation is essential. Drip valves are provided at the lowest points in the train pipe in order to allow for removal of any water droplets which form. These usually comprise a

collection pot with a ball valve at the bottom. Air pressure acting from below keeps the valve closed until the train pipe vacuum is destroyed and then gravity allows the ball to drop thereby releasing any water which has built-up in the pot.

Although most of Britain's steam locomotives were provided with vacuum braking systems the Westinghouse air brake also found application in certain cases. The Westinghouse air brake is very complicated compared with a vacuum system but its operation is worth explaining briefly if only for completeness. Examples in preservation can be seen on the Nene Valley Railway where use of continental air-braked stock requires the fitting of air brakes. The Severn Valley Railway's 'Austerity' 2-10-0 *Gordon* is also equipped for air braking. The only indication of an air-braking arrangement in most cases is the steam operated compressor, fitted to the right-hand side of the smokebox in the case of *Gordon*, with its regular clicking sound as it operates.

In basic terms an air-braked system employs air at 8.28 bar (120 psi) for actuation of the brake cylinders. This air is stored in reservoirs and used to force the pistons of brake cylinders downwards thus applying the brakes via a system of levers. Each item of rolling stock making up the train is provided with a pressure reservoir as well as a brake cylinder. The reservoir is kept charged by means of the pump with the train pipe distributing the air. A triple direction valve is also fitted at each brake position and is actuated by means of pressure in the train pipe. Driver application of the brakes vents the train pipe causing the triple valve to direct air from the reservoir to the cylinder thus applying the brake. Removal of the brakes simply needs pressure in the brake pipe to be restored from the main reservoir and pump. When each brake cylinder is vented powerful springs force the pistons back up their cylinders, thus releasing the brakes.

A requirement of all brake systems is that the brakes will be applied automatically if couplings fail resulting in runaway coaches or wagons. With air brakes that happens because the train pipe will part reducing pressure and the triple valve will direct air from the reservoir to the brake cylinder and so apply the brakes. Advantages claimed for the air brake centre on its more positive action with high loads and the more compact size of cylinders and pipes due to the higher pressure differences involved.

Whether vacuum or air brake operated, cast iron brake shoes exert a braking force on the wheel tyres, that force coming from the brake cylinders through linkages and levers. The single brake cylinder exerts its effort by means of brake rods. In some cases a single rod running down the centre of the locomotive between the wheels connects with brake levers on either side but in other cases brake rods pass down each side of the locomotive to operate shoes on that side only. Which arrangement is used depends upon the designer and also the amount of space between the wheels for such rods. In the case of tenders, which also have all wheels braked from a single cylinder, separate rods had to be used if a water pick-up scoop was provided. All locomotive coupled wheels are braked but with some designs bogie braking was also applied, though problems usually led to the removal of this feature. Braking forces have to be carefully calculated at initial design and need to take account of the total weight of

Diagram of locomotive air brake system.

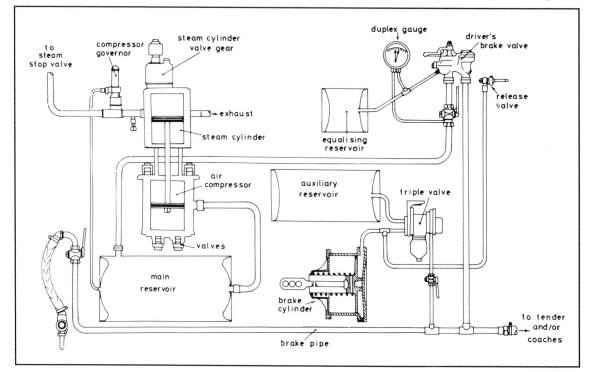

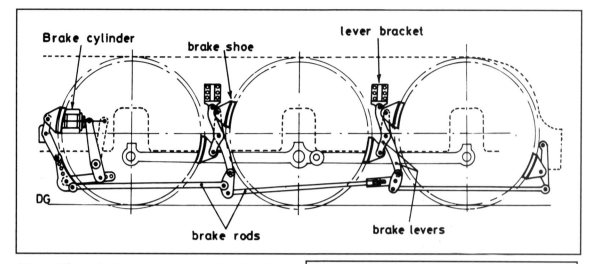

Above *Clasp brake arrangement for Southern Railway 'Pacifics'.*

Right *Arrangement of levers for operating two brake shoes on adjacent wheels using single hanger with clasp brakes.*

locomotive, and tender if fitted. In most cases single blocks on each wheel are sufficient, which is fortunate as systems for applying two brake shoes to each wheel can present problems. It used to be considered also that the application of brake shoes on adjacent wheels from one brake hanger set up stresses in the coupling rods. How true that was is difficult to determine but the system applied with the Bulleid 'Pacifics' worked effectively and without criticism.

The positioning of the brake shoes requires careful consideration as their line of action should be radially towards the wheel centre in order to avoid uneven wear. Shoes should be positioned with centres just above or below the wheel centre so that there is some element of vertical force when the brake is applied. If braking force is applied along the axle centre line it can result in higher axlebox loadings and increased bearing wear. Regular adjustment of the brakes to give equal loading at each wheel is essential in order to ensure optimum braking efficiency. This can be achieved by means of

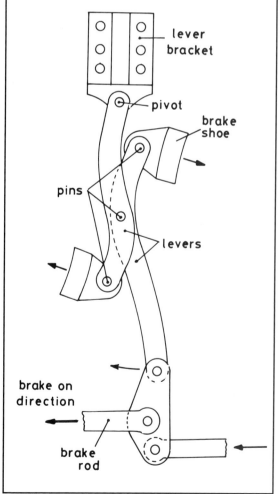

Left *Brake shoe positioning and sand pipe arrangement – plates for balance weights can be seen on the wheel.*

Below right *Steam sanding gear system.*

multi-holed rod ends but the turnbuckle is preferable as it allows for finer adjustment. A handbrake is often provided for use in holding the train at rest in addition to the power brake system and this is achieved by means of a mechanical connection with the brake piston crosshead or brake shaft. This connection takes the form of a slotted link which allows for power operation to bring the train to a halt at which point the handbrake can be applied.

Having brought the locomotive to rest an important aspect of design is to allow it to start again with the minimum of problems. Steel tyres on steel rails do not provide the best of mating surfaces with which to produce a driving force. The coefficient of friction between such surfaces is low, resulting in poor grip. That situation is made worse in wet weather and when oil, grease or wet leaves form a film on the track. Starting a heavy train under such conditions or on a curve or rising gradient can present tremendous problems for the driver, indeed his skill in controlling regulator and cut-off is the only way of ensuring that the train gets away. Designers can provide aids in the form of sanding but careful attention to steam chest pressure and developed cylinder power produces a smooth start under the worst of conditions where a heavy hand on the regulator

will induce slipping even with sanding gear in operation.

Sand between wheels and rails provides grip in the same way that it would for motor car tyres on an icy surface. Delivery of sand in controlled quantities provides for easier starting and climbing of grades under difficult conditions. Dry sanding, allowing sand to be delivered to the rails just in front of the wheels by means of gravity, has advantages not least in simplicity, but with high side winds the sand can be blown away before it can be effective. Steam sanding provides a more positive means of delivery directly to the space between tyre and rail. A steam control valve directs steam to each sanding pipe where a nozzle in the ejector increases the steam velocity. Steam flowing through the nozzle draws air through the pipe and the suction effect of that air passing over the sand trap causes some sand to be sucked into the air flow. Air and sand passing down the pipe is then blown under the driving wheels by the steam jet. This places the sand exactly where it is wanted in limited quantities. In order to allow for reverse running it is usual to fit sanding gear to both sides of the driving wheels but practice differs with designers and company policy.

Many other devices are provided to assist the

easy running of a locomotive although not necessarily for all types. These include such features as sand guns and sootblowers which are intended to keep the firebox and tubes free from deposits. The sand gun is a steam-operated device intended for blasting a jet of sand at the firebox tubeplate at regular intervals whilst the sootblower simply directs a jet of steam at the tubeplate. How effective any of these ideas ever was is difficult to gauge but they were intended to increase the operating period of a locomotive between overhauls and promote more efficient heat transfer.

Locomotives intended for passenger working had to be fitted with a means of supplying steam for carriage heating. As this is really a carriage matter it need not be discussed in any detail save to mention its basic points. Although over the years the different railway companies operating in Britain adopted different systems they had to standardize to some extent in order to allow for the interchange of

stock. For carriage heating a steam pressure of about 3.5 bar (50 psi) is commonly provided, this being supplied from the boiler by means of a reducing valve. Self sealing flexible pipes are used to carry steam from carriage to carriage, individual heating controls being fitted in each compartment or as required. Drain valves in each coach allow for the removal of condensate as it forms thus ensuring that steam and not water flows to the end of the train. The drain valves operate to allow the passage of water only, thus steam leakage is prevented. With an intact system water is drained as it forms and so steam from the reducing valve maintains the desired pressure in the train steam heating pipe at all times. Heating steam pressure can be maintained by setting the reducing valve slightly higher than the maximum pressure allowed in the pipe.

An important duty falling to any footplate crew is that of inspecting the locomotive prior to leaving the shed. In early days and for many

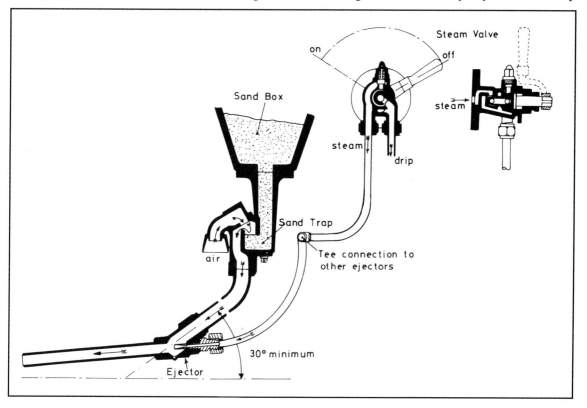

years the use of flares and oil lamps presented the only means of obtaining illumination for such inspections between the frames until some of the more enlightened designers fitted electric lighting to locomotives. Bulleid again was to the fore in this with lamps being provided for headcode duties as well as in the cab and between the frames. A steam-driven turbo-generator was fitted to each of his 'Pacifics', 'Merchant Navy' class locos having it mounted on the running plate below the smokebox whilst for rebuilt 'West Country' machines it can be seen on the left side below the cab.

A feature common to 20th century steam locomotives which found little application on earlier machines is the cab. It does nothing for the operation of the locomotive but provides valuable comfort for the footplate crew, especially in cold and wet weather. Designers of early steam locomotives paid scant regard to the well-being of drivers and firemen, considering them to be hardy folk who could stand the elements, but some of their 20th century counterparts offered little improvement. Protection from the elements and seats found little favour with certain designers, Churchward on the GWR being notable for his basic cab amenities. In later years matters improved and footplate crews experienced better weather protection. Even then, however, running tender first could be particularly uncomfortable. The provision of accommodation for the crew was

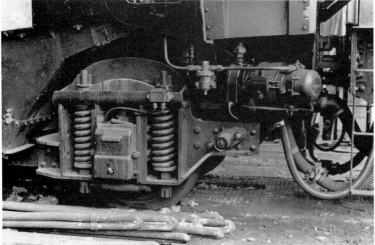

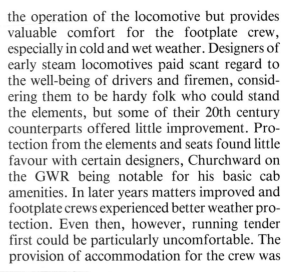

Left *'West Country' 'Pacific' showing position of electrical generator and pony truck design. Superheater tubes can be seen in the foreground.*

Below *Two types of 0-6-0 tank locomotives exhibiting variations in tank and cab arrangements. Midland design '1F' No 41708 and Riddles Austerity tank posing as 'J94' Class No 68012.*

Above right *Southern eight-wheeled tender as fitted to Urie 'S15' No 506.*

always a compromise between all-round protection and the need for clear visibility to be maintained.

Tender locomotives cannot be provided with completely enclosed cabs but in certain cases a weatherboard in the tender offered a degree of protection. Ivatt-designed LMS 2–6–0s made good use of such a feature which found its way onto many BR standard tender locomotives. Canvas weather protection covers, known as storm sheets, stretched between cab roof and tender were the best that many footplate crews could hope for and in driving rain they offered little enough protection. It is astonishing that fundamental devices such as folding cabside doors failed to find general acceptance right up to nationalization although there were also a number of designers who appeared to make every effort to ensure the comfort of footplate crews. Although it has to be said that some drivers preferred to drive from the standing position it is self evident that comfortable seating must have been a blessing on a long run. Comparison between the standard of comfort offered by Bulleid on his Southern Railway 'Pacifics' with that of GWR locos built during the same 1940s period illustrates the difference and the reader is recommended to inspect the footplate of 'West Country' and 'Manor' Classes if the opportunity presents itself.

Tender

As far as the locomotive designer was concerned this piece of rolling stock was a necessary evil. It carried coal and water but did nothing to assist in power production, with the rare exception of devices like the Sturrock tender driving engine. Although the function of a tender is simple, considerable thought had to be given to its design in order to suit it to a particular locomotive. Water and coal capacity are obvious considerations but operating speed and the drawbar pull of the locomotive played an important part in overall design. Efficient braking is also essential, usually forming part of the vacuum system even where a steam brake is provided for the locomotive.

Although six-wheeled tenders seemed to predominate in British practice some railways, especially the Southern, had a preference for eight wheels on tenders and even the use of bogies. Coal capacity varies with locomotive type and class but bunker sides and floor are made with a slope in order to allow coal to fall naturally to the front. That at least was the design intention but it did not always work that way and firemen were frequently forced to work at the back of the tender to force coal forward. The adoption of the steam-operated coal pusher in some designs removed that

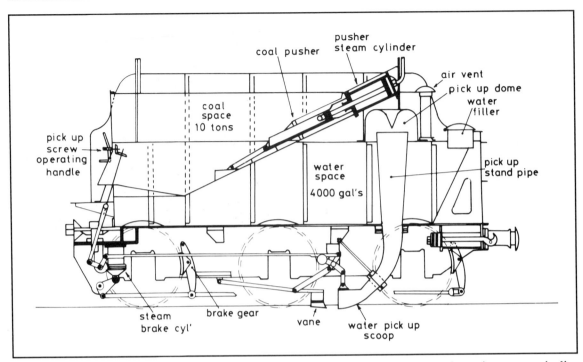

necessity. Consisting basically of a flat plate connected to a rod which could be moved by means of a steam cylinder it was not commonly fitted in British practice but the device did find favour with the LMS for its 'Duchess' Class 'Pacifics' and the preserved *Duchess of Hamilton* still has an operational device. The un-mistakable blast from exhausting steam indicates when it is working.

A more commonly fitted device though for a different purpose and rarely seen on Southern locomotives was the water pick-up apparatus. Although no longer used in preservation a number of tenders are still fitted with their

Above *LMS large tender showing water scoop, steam brake and coal pusher.*

Left *Water scoop still fitted to preserved GWR 2-8-0 locomotive.*

Right *Preserved BR Standard '9F' No 92203,* Black Prince, *showing tender with inset coal bunker allowing for better rear viewing.*

water scoops. The principle of operation is that at speed (not excessive) the scoop could be lowered so that it came below the water level of an approaching water trough laid between the rails. Velocity alone would cause the water to be forced up the scoop into the tender, a dome being provided to dissipate water energy. In most cases guide vanes were fitted just before the scoop in order to control the entry of water and so avoid excessive splashing from the trough. When the required quantity of water had been taken the fireman would raise the scoop by means of a screw mechanism but if he was not quick enough the tender tank could overflow and water flowing out of the air vents would wash the leading coach! Should anybody be unfortunate, or inexperienced, enough to occupy the front compartment with its windows open when passing over water troughs a degree of dampness might be experienced. Unfortunately no operating water troughs exist in preservation to demonstrate the arrangement which allowed long non-stop runs to be made during the heyday of steam traction. A number of tank locomotives were actually provided with reversible water scoops which could be operated whilst the locomotive was running in either direction. Again the feature only found favour with certain de-

'Castle' Class locomotive picking up water with considerable overflow. (D.K. Jones Collection)

signers. By contrast no method of taking on coal while on the move was ever introduced into service.

Although it might seem that a tender is little more than a simple water tank on wheels which could also carry coal, detailed aspects of the design could make a lot of difference to locomotive performance. Baffles in the water space, for example, prevent water from washing from side to side or end to end with a

motion which could induce instability, but the water must still drain when required. The shape of a tender depends primarily upon its designed water and coal capacity but space must always be provided for stowing fire irons and other tools. Good design should also allow the driver and fireman a clear view down the tender sides, a vital requirement when running tender first. Many of the BR standard tenders had inset bunker spaces which allowed for better viewing.

For its non-stop runs to the north the LNER provided some of its 'Pacifics' with corridor tenders thus allowing for a footplate crew change en route. The narrow corridor down one side of the tender occupied space which would normally have been taken by water but the loss of capacity was minimal and could be made up by taking water from troughs during the run. The round window glass for the corridor can still be seen on the tenders of some LNER preserved 'Pacifics'.

CHAPTER 5

Locomotive types

The distance a locomotive can travel non-stop is determined by its water and fuel capacity, as well as its ability to take on water while under way. Smokebox cleaning and other routine operations to ensure efficient running dictates the maximum distance a locomotive might run without a trip to the sheds. In Britain the longest run of this type was between London and Scotland with LMS and LNER 'Pacifics' being designed accordingly. Tenders with coal capacity for the journey and even corridors for crew changes allowed for such long distance runs.

In terms of design and operation stowing coal and water on the locomotive itself, as opposed to a tender, had many advantages, not least being the fact that it avoided the need for a costly appendage to be dragged behind. Coal and water carried in this way added to the adhesive weight of the engine making for increased assurance against slipping but did present problems in that stowage took up space and made certain parts more difficult to reach. Storage capacity, particularly for coal, was more limited than was possible with a tender though water could, of course, be picked up from troughs if the correct gear was fitted. Limited coal capacity, carried in a bunker at

Passenger tender locomotives of different pattern: LMS design 'Patriot' Class 4-6-0 No 45519, Lady Godiva, *and LNER design 'A3' 4-6-2 No 60085,* Manna. *(D.K. Jones Collection)*

Left *Austerity 0-6-0 saddle tank No 69 as preserved on the Yorkshire Dales Railway.*

Right *Standard Class '4MT' 2-6-4 tank No 80079. An example of how styling applied to tanks could improve appearance.*

Below right *Lancashire and Yorkshire Railway Aspinall-designed 0-6-0 tender freight locomotive – the high dome characterised many late nineteenth-century boilers.*

the rear of the cab, effectively limited the operating distance of tank locomotives. The tank locomotive, without the burden of a tender came into its own where regular reversing of train direction was part of normal operations — on branch lines, for example, where tank locomotive designs could run in either direction with a degree of convenience which tender-first running could never achieve.

Thus express passenger locomotives and those designed for long-distance freight services had to be of the tender type, whilst for shunting, station pilot and short branch line working the tank engine sufficed. There are always exceptions to any classification but this situation applied to most railways in Britain. Between these two extremes there existed a wide band of locomotive sizes and wheel arrangements where tenders and tanks found equal employment. In fact, tender and tank versions of the same design were often produced.

Side tanks, well tanks, pannier tanks and saddle tanks were all used for the carriage of water although the rear cab coal bunker space never seemed to vary. There was never any definite evidence that one form of tank was any better than other types and tradition as much as anything else determined this aspect of locomotive design. Pannier tanks became something of a GWR trademark and few people

would associate them with any other railway. The fact that they remained part of GWR design for so many years indicates a degree of satisfaction, but much the same could be said for side tanks on LMS locos and saddle tanks on industrial types. An important feature of design however required that tanks on either side of the boiler be interconnected in order to maintain lateral equilibrium and allow for the even distribution of weight. Positioning of the tanks also played an important part in stability since too much weight high up could be destabilizing, especially at speed. Careful design dictated that the desired water capacity be achieved from a combination of length, height and width of tank whilst the locomotive remained within the loading gauge. Well tanks positioned below the boiler made it possible to reduce the capacity of side tanks, lower the centre of gravity and so obtain a considerable increase in stability.

Adhesive weight, basically that weight of a locomotive resting on the driving wheels, is an important factor in engine design. The higher its value the greater the locomotive's ability to haul loads without risk of slipping. If no bogies or pony trucks are fitted then all the weight is carried on the driving wheels making for increased pulling capability, which is especially important when starting. Set limits for axle loadings however, especially on bridges, dictate

how many coupled wheels must be used in order to distribute that adhesive weight. Increased power generation, i.e. hauling capacity, usually required a heavier locomotive. Whereas an 0–4–0 arrangement may be useful for light shunting duties the small size of such a locomotive does not provide sufficient power generation for hauling heavier loads. The 0–6–0 arrangement certainly became the most popular in Britain for steady and sure-footed goods work. Higher tractive effort require-

ments necessitated heavier locomotives which could not be carried on three axles within weight restrictions hence development of the 0–8–0 wheel arrangement. Although 0–6–0s were of tank or tender design in almost equal proportions, the 0–8–0 arrangement was almost exclusively the domain of the tender type.

The size and number of wheels was similarly dictated by a number of restrictions but there has never been any set rule which governs practice for all locomotive designs. Weight

restrictions on bridges etc. certainly imposed a limit with respect to axle loading but weight may be distributed amongst driving wheels, bogies and pony trucks. Only driving wheels, however, transmit any tractive force and carrying wheels were often required for other reasons. Decisions regarding the number of driving and other wheels could not be made in an arbitrary manner in order to suit appearance, each axle was provided for a particular purpose.

At higher speeds a heavy locomotive needed to be guided in order to allow safe and easy movement into and out of curves as well as over points and crossings. The bogie or pony truck provided that degree of flexibility which is essential in order to avoid heavy forces being imposed on the flanges of driving wheels. Different types of bogies, including several radial forms, have been devised over the years in order to provide such easy transition into and out of curves and all worked effectively to a greater or lesser extent. Correct springing is the main factor that determines how well bogies provide the correct degree of guiding force to the locomotive frame, and hence the driving wheels: rough riding resulted from excessive stiffness. With new designs trial and error was often the only means of obtaining the correct guiding effect.

On locomotives intended for lower speeds carrying wheels often took the form of a pony truck with a single axle rather than a twin-axled bogie. The overall reasoning and effect was the same, to guide the locomotive into and out of curves. In general the higher the operational speed the greater the requirement for a bogie but no hard and fast single speed determined whether a pony truck or bogies should be used. At the rear of the locomotive, carrying wheels, again pony truck or bogie, could be used to support some of the locomotive's weight if firebox width prevented the fitting of large diameter driving wheels in that position. In Britain the pony truck found favour for tender locomotives but bogies had to be used for a number of tank designs due to the large over-

hang formed by an extended cab and the requirement to run fast in reverse almost as frequently as forward. Again it depended upon size and no definite rules applied. In certain cases, such as the standard '9Fs', a wide firebox boiler could be fitted without the provision of rear carrying wheels. This became possible because the boiler was pitched high to the loading gauge limit and driving wheel diameter was not excessively large.

The size of the driving wheels governs tractive effort (measured in lb force) in the standard Phillipson formula:

$$\text{Tractive effort} = \frac{0.85 \, d^2 \, s \, n \, p}{2w}$$

where d = cylinder diameter (inches)
       s = piston stroke (inches)
       n = number of cylinder
       p = boiler pressure (psi)
       w = driving wheel diameter (inches)

The above equation is for two cylinders; for three and four cylinders multiplying factors of 1.5 and 2 respectively must be used.

Tractive effort is rather a vague, and even arbitrary, concept in that it does not denote the locomotive's actual power. It does, however, give some indication as to the ability to haul, or rather start, loads.

Driving wheel diameter must be arranged to suit a particular maximum locomotive speed and desired maximum piston speed. As discussed in Chapter 3 there is a definite time required for steam to flow through valve passages into the cylinder. Should a piston be moving too quickly steam chases it and no energy is transmitted. Apart from running down hill, when steam would be shut off anyway, this situation cannot happen as it is the steam which gives the piston its motion but at high piston speeds the full steam force will not be exerted on the piston and power potential will be lost. Reasonable piston speeds must be maintained especially if steam is to be directed to the cylinder for a large portion of the stroke

Dean single wheeler No 3063, Duke of York, *at Exeter about 1900.* (Courtesy of the National Railway Museum, York)

as is often the case with slow moving goods engines. Higher speed passenger locos make extensive use of expansive working and so less steam needs to flow to the cylinder on each stroke.

For a set maximum piston speed, and hence wheel rotational speed with a given crank length, the locomotive's speed then is determined by wheel diameter. It follows that higher locomotive speeds can be obtained from larger diameter wheels, hence for express passenger locomotives larger diameter driving wheels are used. The situation is similar to the gearing on a bicycle or car: at high ratios the vehicle goes faster for the same pedal or engine speed. At low ratios the vehicle moves more slowly but has increased hauling power, such as when climbing hills. From this it should follow that smaller diameter wheels are of use for slower moving locomotives which need to start and pull heavy loads. This is the case with the goods engine. Other factors also need to be considered, not least the effect of centrifugal force on large diameter high-speed wheels, if this is too high and the wheel/tyre strength insuffi-

cient then bursting might take place. The balance of reciprocating masses, as discussed on page 76, was also an important design consideration.

Having decided upon driving wheel diameter and the need, or otherwise, for carrying wheels there remained the matter of how many driving wheels had to be provided. The number of driving axles must suit the power being transmitted and at the same time allow for reasonable loading on the track. Both depend, to some extent, upon the locomotive's size. The transmission of higher powers, especially when starting, can result in slipping but the introduction of sanding gear reduced that effect giving an extension to the use of the single wheelers. In simple terms, the higher the power to be transmitted the greater the number of driving wheels needed. Axle loading can be reduced by the provision of carrying wheels but pony trucks or bogies also reduce adhesion since the entire weight of the locomotive is then not acting through the driving wheels.

In the end design is always somewhat of a compromise. Basic requirements are to keep

below maximum allowed axle loading, paying due regard to hammer blow, whilst transmitting desired power from the cylinders and maintaining high adhesive weight. Bearing this in mind the designer could produce an 0–6–0, 2–6–0 ('Mogul'), 2–6–2 ('Prairie'), 4–4–2 ('Atlantic'), 4–6–2 ('Pacific'), or any other arrangement which fitted his requirements and prevailing restrictions. There were certainly fashions in wheel arrangement but this probably followed particular power demands and changes in axle loading restrictions which appear to have changed for most railways in Britain at about the same time. It is highly unlikely that any designer adopted a particular arrangement mostly because it looked attractive or photogenic. The prestige brought about by being responsible for Britain's first 'Atlantic', 'Pacific', 2–8–0, or other such wheel arrangement may have entered the mind of

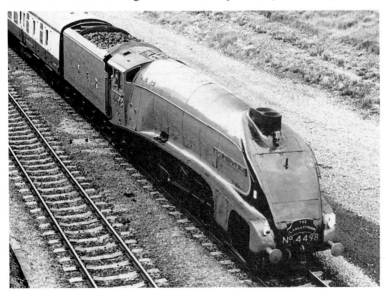

Above The 4–4–0 arrangement illustrated by Drummond 'T9' Class No 30304, built in 1901. (D.K. Jones Collection)

Left LNER streamlining: preserved 'A4' Sir Nigel Gresley.

Right LMS streamlining: No 6222, Queen Mary, on the down Coronation Scot near Tamworth. (Courtesy of the National Railway Museum, York)

individual designers but they were professionals serving the needs of their employers and they are unlikely to have even thought of engaging in such ephemeral competition. Competition to produce a better locomotive, however, was a different matter.

In the eyes of many, including railway company directors, better meant faster and the search for speed grew apace in the 1920s and 1930s. Streamlining became much in vogue as a means of reducing drag due to air resistance. Wind tunnel tests certainly showed that Gresley's streamlined 'A4''Pacifics' required less power at high speeds than a machine without an outer casing. How effective such casings were in practice is difficult now to prove but they must have been less effective than those tests showed. Side winds and the anomalous effects of air movement in cuttings and on embankments must have reduced the advantage claimed for streamlining and at reduced speeds it was much lower anyway. Casings made maintenance more difficult and the fact that Collett's experiment on the GWR was short lived and all streamlined Stanier 'Pacifics' were subsequently de-streamlined indicates that for British conditions the disadvantages outweighed the advantages in practical terms. From the publicity point of view,

however, a streamlined locomotive had much to commend it during the 1930s.

Improved efficiency on the steam generating side could often be gained, or destroyed, by the fireman but some designers did attempt to produce devices which sought to help by, for example, removing some of the energy from the chimney exhaust to heat up boiler feed. It has already been mentioned that hot water supplied to an injector would stop it working but heating the water on its way from injector to boiler had advantages. Apart from steam employed for the exhaust steam injector there was little use in taking further steam for feed heating as that could reduce the blast effect. Waste heat in the chimney gases could be employed for heating boiler water and one of the most widely used devices was the Crosti heater. Experimental application to some standard '9Fs' did not produce the improvements expected and the devices were subsequently removed.

In basic terms the Crosti heater consisted of a cylindrical vessel positioned below the boiler. Water was supplied to the unit from the injectors and heated by exhaust gas passing through tubes. This gas passed to a final smokebox and was discharged through a rectangular form chimney on the right-hand side

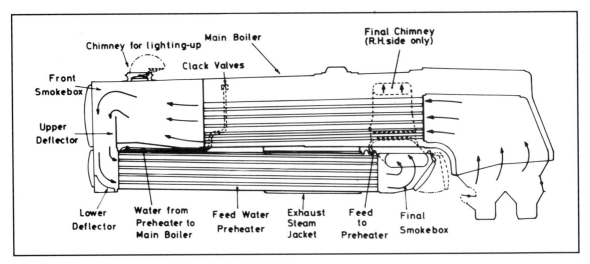

Chimney for lighting-up
Main Boiler
Final Chimney (R.H.side only)
Clack Valves
Front Smokebox
Upper Deflector
Lower Deflector
Water from Preheater to Main Boiler
Feed Water Preheater
Exhaust Steam Jacket
Feed to Preheater
Final Smokebox

Diagram of Crosti boiler arrangement.

of the locomotive. An exhaust steam jacket surrounding part of the heater also provided some heat to the feed water. That the experiment proved less of a success than hoped is unfortunate. It may be that the designers were too optimistic but, as with the trials involving mechanical stokers, the fitted '9Fs' never regularly operated on the long runs with heavy trains for which they were designed and so, perhaps, the trials were never representative of their service potential.

Main lines in Britain were invariably constructed to high standards and the need for locomotive designs of other than 'normal' forms were few and far between. The same cannot be said for overseas railways or narrow gauge lines which had individual requirements of high power or the need to negotiate sharp curves. Over the years several designs were produced, some with more success than others. This is no place to discuss in detail the world's stranger steam locomotives but mention of some is worthwhile, especially those which found service in Britain.

LMS Garratt No 4999. (Courtesy of the National Railway Museum, York)

Articulated locomotives allowed high power machines to be built for lines with low axle loading requirements and relatively sharp curves. A number of different designs achieved this aim but the most successful was the Garratt. A single locomotive of this type was constructed for operation on the LNER but 33 Garratts of 2–6–0 + 0–6–2 form were built for the LMS. Several smaller industrial Garratts were also built for service in the UK.

The Garratt concept embodies two powered bogie units with a boiler mounted between them using pivots. The power unit at the boiler cab end carries a coal bunker and water tank whilst a further water tank is placed on the power unit at the chimney end. Because the boiler is placed between both sets of driving wheels the size of the boiler does not restrict wheel size. The boiler may be positioned relatively low down and can, therefore, be made with as large a diameter as the loading gauge will allow. A large diameter short boiler is ideal for efficient steam generation provided that the firebox has been correctly sized. Two power units provide large power outputs and that power may be transmitted through any desired number of driving wheels to suit axle loading restrictions. Garratts also have the advantage of tank locomotives in that the weight of water and coal is on the driving wheels and so assist with adhesion.

The good quality track with few sharp curves and reasonable axle loading allowances which existed on Britain's main lines meant that Garratt locomotives were never able to prove their true worth since conventional high-powered machines were well capable of operating within the restrictions. Conditions on many lines abroad were not so reasonable and Garratts could be found in large numbers on railways in all five continents. South Africa made early and extensive use of the concept both for its standard gauge lines, 1067 mm (3 ft 6 in), and narrow gauge lines, 610 mm (2 ft). The Beyer Peacock built 4–8–2 + 2–8–4 'GL' Class Garratts weighed in at over 218 tonnes (214 tons) and were amongst the most powerful

steam locomotives ever constructed in Britain with a tractive effort of 78,650 lb. By comparison the 60,700 lb tractive effort of the South African 'GMA' and 'GMAM' Class Garratts seems almost puny but their axle loading of less than 16.29 tonnes (16 tons) allowed for more widespread operations. It has to be remembered that these machines, more powerful than an LMS 'Duchess' in terms of tractive effort, were designed to operate on sharply curved track of 3 ft 6 in gauge. In them the concept has certainly reached its zenith.

The Mallet articulated locomotive with its pivoted powered bogie unit and rigid frame never found application in Britain but the Fairlie format did. The Festiniog Railway put the design to use and two of its double Fairlies may still be seen in regular operation, although one is of recent construction. The concept is similar to that of the Garratt with pivoted power units being placed each end of the locomotive. In the case of the double Fairlies there is a single boiler with two separate fireboxes in the centre of the locomotive and chimneys at each end. The long boiler unit on its frame is rigid but bogies pivot to allow the negotiation of sharp curves.

Although variations in power unit arrangement and disposition have been fairly plentiful these units have generally been of the reciprocating type, the only competitor being in the form of the steam turbine. Unfortunately the turbine does not lend itself to rail traction and so the limited applications made no real inroads on traditional drives. Two basic problems exist as far as turbine drives are concerned, these being the fact that a turbine operates at high speed, thus gearing is essential, and the fact that it is not reversible, thus a reverse turbine is needed. These facts do not make turbine drives any less efficient, in fact thermodynamically a turbine drive is more efficient than a reciprocating drive, but they added to the capital cost and increased the complexity.

Advantages of a turbine drive include the avoidance of unbalanced reciprocating masses

Festiniog Railway double Fairlie Merddin Emrys, *built in 1879.*

because there are no pistons, thus there is no hammer blow. Lubrication problems existing at crossheads, connecting rods and valve gear are also eliminated because these parts are absent. Turbines do not require any lubrication of the working parts, except for gearing and bearings, and so the problem of cylinder and valve lubrication with superheated steam is eliminated. Britain's most successful turbine locomotive, and it was a success in operation although its unique nature kept route and applications very limited, was the LMS 'Pacific' No 6202, known as the Turbomotive. It is important to remember that there was an alternative to the reciprocating steam engine but any non-standard type of drive would have had to be substantially better than that already existing. The cost of change in terms of crew training, spares provision and different repair facilities never proved to be justified and the mass changeover from steam to diesel and electric power never gave such innovations a chance.

Steam turbines aboard ship and in power stations work to high efficiencies because they can make maximum use of steam energy down to very low absolute pressures. Some form of condenser is required and this could never be effectively provided for a railway locomotive, although several condensing turbine locos were produced. With steam condensed to produce low turbine back pressure, higher power output should be expected but in the case of a locomotive exhaust steam is used to produce a draught. A smokebox fan will provide an 'artificial' draught but at the expense of added complication.

The only effective condenser developed for a steam locomotive was that fitted to the South African Class '25s'. This was to preserve water whilst operating in the vast wastes of the Great Karoo semi-desert rather than to assist a turbine, since a two-cylinder reciprocating drive of conventional form applied to the '25s'. A massive tender housed the air-cooled condenser unit, use of which reduced water consumption by 60 per cent. Steam turbines to drive the fans developed 410 kW (550 hp) whilst that for inducing smokebox draught produced 112 kW (150hp). Condensing locomotives have been designed for operation in the UK but they were for tunnel duties, essentially the London Underground and Mersey Railway. In these cases no special condensing unit was fitted exhaust steam simply being directed to the water tanks. Naturally, operation in this mode was limited in order to avoid water boiling in the storage tanks.

Mountain-climbing locomotives provide another variation on the same basic reciprocating engine theme but these produce a rail drive by means of a rack rather than by wheels running on smooth rails. The system used on Britain's Snowdon Mountain railway has the rack between the two rails. Apart from the drive and sloping boiler these machines are essentially the same in principle as that developed by the Stephensons.

The same can really be said for most steam locomotive designs except, perhaps, the few turbine drives. Details changed and complexity increased but a boiler still produced steam which was used to drive wheels by means of pistons working in cylinders. It is quite amazing that such a relatively simple engineering concept should last so long, with but few major variations, until the steam locomotive ceased commercial railway operations.

CHAPTER 6.

Driving and firing

Whatever the type or size of steam locomotive one factor remained very much the same. Footplate crew comprised a fireman and a driver. The nature of locomotive work might have differed from shunting to express passenger operations but that expected of the crew did not. The fireman's job remained the maintenance of a steam supply for the driver to make use of in carrying out the duties required. That situation still exists on preserved railways. Although oil firing has been used from time to time the description of the crew's role on the footplate given here will relate to manual coal firing because of its more widespread application.

Over the years a great many books have been written by former footplate personnel, each relating that person's experiences with different types of locomotive and services. I do not intend to cover that same ground, an impossibility anyway as there is such a wide variety of locomotives to be considered. I intend instead to deal with the fundamentals of good and safe footplate operations, avoiding specific consideration of any one particular locomotive class or run. The point all of these published volumes of footplate reminiscences make is that the good crew was always a team with each member being able to co-operate with the other and anticipate situations likely to result in changes in operation.

In basic terms the fireman's task is to ensure an adequate supply of steam at the correct pressure in order to meet the demands of the driver. That might appear to be a fairly straightforward task, and on paper it is, but out on the line the reality imposes problems. Heat from coal cannot be made available immediately as it can with a gas burner: it takes time for coal to burn and liberate its heat. From this it follows that an increased steam supply is not available at the flick of a switch, unlike electricity. Although the driver does the driving the fireman still requires an awareness of the road's gradients for these dictate the amount of power required at any particular time. To wait until the train is on a gradient with steam pressure falling before commencing to fire is to invite adverse comment from the driver. Firing for a particular gradient has to commence some time before it is reached and the likely steam demand is also affected by whether a heavy or light train is being worked.

Too much steam results in waste as the safety valves lift. This is not only a waste of coal and water but a waste of effort on the part of the fireman for his work with the shovel is simply going towards making patterns in the sky. The good fireman will anticipate the end of a climb or approach of a falling gradient and adjust his firing accordingly. At the end of a long run firing may cease many miles before the terminal station is reached, the burning coals in the firebox being capable of producing sufficient steam to complete the run and allow movement to the shed for disposal. The locomotive could then arrive on shed with its fire well down in the firebox, resulting in less waste and an easier job for those responsible for dropping the fire. Even if the locomotive goes back into service after cleaning and checking, the fire would still be allowed to burn down as that made cleaning and removal of clinker a much easier task.

Firing on the road is more than simply putting shovel after shovel of coal into the firebox and the task has never been easy. Apart from the hard physical effort of the job great care has to be taken in building and maintaining a fire, heaping layer upon layer of coal is not enough. Firebox shape dictates the way in which a fire needs to be formed and maintained whilst the grade of coal being burnt also has to be taken into consideration. Each case and each fire has to be dealt with as an individual and no complete rules could be applied throughout even where firebox shape and grate size were similar.

In a deep flat firebox where a large air space was provided between the firebars a deep fire would be appropriate. Firing technique differed with individual firemen but the maintenance of an even fire was all important. A number of shovels in the corners then along each side and finally in the middle usually satisfies the flat grate. Obviously the interval between firing also has to be such as to maintain an even fire. If the air space between the firebars is on the small side a thin fire has to be employed in order to ensure that the burning coals receive adequate air. Long sloping grates can be fired more readily as coal placed near the door should be shaken down towards the front by vibration. Care always had to be taken in steam days to ensure that this was actually taking place otherwise an uneven fire with holes might result. With this type of firebox, coal was generally applied at the sides and under the door but not at the front.

Wide fireboxes with sloping grates, as fitted to 'Pacifics', could only be effectively fired by keeping the back corners and the space under the door well filled and allowing vibration to shift the coal to the front. It took, and still takes on preserved lines, an experienced fireman to manage the situation in order to produce steam as required by the driver. Dexterity with the shovel, whether the small or large type, comes only from practice and a good fireman in steam days could place a quantity of coal exactly where he wanted with the minimum of effort. The inexperienced man had a much harder task. It is not simply a case of brute force but a careful swing and a deft twist of the wrist is necessary to allow the coal to fall on the designated spot. No amount of descriptive writing can explain that art or that of 'reading the fire' to see where the fuel is needed. The uninitiated should try throwing a spadeful of garden earth to a precise spot some 2 m to 3 m away in order to realise the task facing the fireman. It then has to be remembered that the fireman had to perform that task regularly over many hours on a rather unsteady platform and direct the shovel through the very narrow gap which was the firebox door. What appears to be a pleasant and even appealing job in the context of a preserved railway was often far from that during the days of main line steam. Shifting coal for hours on end whilst being frozen and soaked during winter or roasted in the heat of summer was never the truly glamorous job that many would like to believe. Firing a steam locomotive was hard, dirty, demanding and skilled work.

Good combustion is also efficient combustion and not only saves coal but also reduces the firemans's work load for he has to shovel less. Coal is a compound material consisting of carbon, hydrogen, sulphur, ash, and other substances. Carbon accounts for between 70 and 90 per cent of the mass and, therefore, produces most of the heat when the coal burns. The way in which a particular type of coal burns depends upon the relative proportions of its constituent materials. The more volatile substances vaporize when coal is added to a fire and burn in the form of a luminous flame. This takes place where hydrogen is present as hydrogen combines with carbon to form combustible

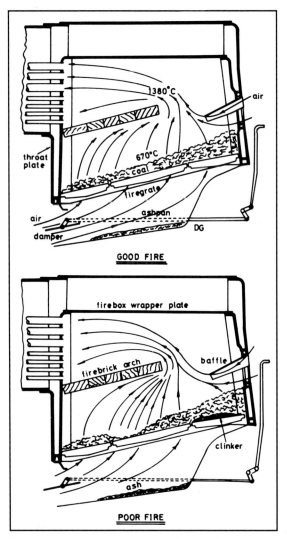

Diagrams comparing good and poor fires.

hydrocarbon vapours. Coal such as anthracite contains very little hydrogen and is unsuitable for burning in a conventional firebox which is designed for combustion of volatile vapours. Yellowish smoke issuing from a locomotive chimney consists mostly of hydrocarbon vapours which have not burnt. Black smoke is carbon which results from partial combustion of these vapours: only the hydrogen has burnt.

The main requirement of good combustion is that coal, when added to a previously clear fire, forms hydrocarbon vapours which mix with air and burn completely. The air is drawn up through the fire and also enters above the fire through the fire door. Correct regulation of air flow from both sources is essential to ensure efficient combustion. When sufficient air is supplied carbon forms carbon dioxide, hydrogen forms water vapour and sulphur forms sulphur trioxide. It is essential, however, to ensure that the fire base is maintained at the correct temperature to liberate the volatile vapours. If the fire cools then these vapours are not effectively released and combustion is not complete. Low temperatures come about if the fire is too deep or has become shallow in places, thus allowing a cooling draught of air to pass through the fire from below. A build-up of clinker can restrict air flow through the fire and also reduce fire temperature by preventing the premixing between volatile vapours and oxygen.

Air supply above the fire allows for complete combustion of the volatile vapours, or more particularly the carbon monoxide which forms. Although complete combustion produces carbon dioxide it is carbon monoxide which forms first from the air coming in below the fire, the secondary air from above allows for more complete combustion and full liberation of heat. Careful control of air supply from below and above the fire is, therefore, essential to efficient combustion and maintenance of steam pressure. Too little air from either source results in smoke and less heat being liberated, whilst too much air has the effect of cooling down the flue gas temperature resulting in lower heat transfer to the water. It is the fireman's job to ensure that the correct quantity of air, no more and no less, is supplied. The air supply must suit his rate of firing and also the type of coal being burnt. Use of the damper and firebox door openings allow air supply above and below the fire to be regulated. Strength of draught must be considered alongside the amount of opening. With some types of coal it can be difficult to determine when the correct amount of air is being supplied. The usual rule of just allowing the smoke to disappear is fine with many types but certain types are practically smokeless. With these the fire has to be watched carefully for any change in colour or condition. The quality of the coal used dictates the amount of impurity present and impurities produces clinker on the firebars. With poor quality coal considerable amounts of clinker can be expected and the fireman's job becomes very difficult as he must break up the clinker in order to obtain a clear air path through the bars. In such circumstances there is little to be done except indulge in plenty of hard work, but fire and fireman both suffer.

In main line service knowledge of the road allowed a fireman to adjust his firing rate and water supply in order to provide maximum pressure just when required. Too early resulted in blowing off, too late and speed suffered.

Station and possible signal checks, as well as mandatory speed restrictions all had to be borne in mind and the firing rate adjusted accordingly. Factors such as unexpected signal checks or delayed departure from a station could always upset the best laid plans of the most meticulous fireman. Boiler water level and steam pressure would be just right as booked departure time came around but any delay inevitably resulted in wasteful blowing off, and no fireman had any control over that.

Whilst at a stand damper controls could be operated in order to reduce air flow and water could be forced into the boiler if the level was not already at a maximum. Any cold feed would absorb heat and so delay the point at which blowing off occurred but a good fireman would already have had the correct water level

A locomotive steaming well – No 6000, King George V, *on Gresford Bank.*

if the train had been standing at a station for any time. Out on the road matters might be somewhat different but the maintenance of a minimum water level was essential. Uncovering of the furnace crown had catastrophic consequences.

It is difficult to deal with exact circumstances as they differed with run, load and the steaming capabilities of a particular locomotive. For level or downhill running the injectors could readily maintain water level but when pulling hard uphill a conflict always existed between steam demand for propulsion and steam for water injection. Although an exhaust steam injector may have been available this might not have been capable of supplying sufficient water to maintain level. At times a fireman, and his driver, might need to keep their fingers crossed that the summit would be reached before water disappeared from the glass.

Careful use of live and exhaust steam injectors allowed water level to be kept within limits but a good fireman would always ensure that he had a full glass and well stocked fire if a stretch of heavy gradient was imminent. Again this required knowledge of the road. Operation of injectors has already been discussed but it is worth mentioning that at times a fireman had to battle in order to get one or other of the two operational. Whilst on a run the exhaust steam injector was most frequently used with the live steam unit being operated when stationary or drifting. A temperamental exhaust steam injector meant that total reliance rested with the live steam injector. Because many exhaust steam injectors gave trouble BR standard classes were fitted with two live steam units rather than one of each type. Regular blowing of the gauge glass ensured that it was reading correctly.

A fireman's duties extended further than feeding coal into a firebox and maintaining water level however. Depending upon circumstances he may have had to deal with coaling of the tender or otherwise ensure that the coal was safely stowed and that loose lumps were unlikely to fall off and cause injury. The same applied to the stowage of fire-irons. In dry weather dust from coal could cause considerable inconvenience in the cab and a spray with water at regular intervals would minimize the spread of dust. Washing down of the cab with water also fell to the fireman. Following arrival on shed after a run it was usual to coal and water a locomotive prior to movement to the ash pit for cleaning of the fire. A further essential duty which fell to the fireman was removal of char from the smokebox. Even with self-cleaning smokeboxes a certain amount of char would remain in the smokebox and require disposal. Any char which fell on the loco front had to be swept away: it was not only unsightly but could cause injury when the locomotive returned to service. Pieces of char blowing into the eyes of footplate crew, passengers or anybody near the lineside might have serious consequences.

A strict demarcation of footplate duties was never found on the railways of Britain as much depended upon the regulations of each company and upon the whims of individual drivers. Under most circumstances it fell to the fireman to ensure that the locomotive was provided with a full set of fire-irons, tools, lamps, detonators, rags, oil cans, etc. prior to leaving the shed. A quantity of engine and lamp oil also had to be collected. Oiling around the locomotive could also be entrusted to some firemen whilst certain drivers might only trust themselves to do that job. Whatever the instructions regarding actual oiling or the making of trimmings for oil pots the duty had to be performed carefully and correctly in accordance with the requirements of a particular locomotive. This is where real teamwork became a footplate art as the driver knew exactly what he could trust his fireman to do.

What has been written above is in no way intended to be a training manual for would-be firemen, it merely gives an outline of the basic duties and essential features of the job. There are many books relating footplate experiences and these may be consulted for information regarding individual recollections of main line

'Black Five' No 45000, with char below the smokebox after cleaning - a potential cause of injury. (D.K. Jones Collection)

operations.

The driver was in charge of the footplate and so responsible for everything which took place with respect to the locomotive and its ability to haul the train. Timekeeping formed an important part of his duties and he had to ensure that the train kept to booked time throughout its journey and also operated safely. Knowledge of the road with its signals, gradients and speed restrictions was an essential part of his job whilst adherence to these restrictions and signals was a mandatory requirement. When booking on the driver had to ensure that he knew and understood any notices relevant to his route, train and locomotive. His job card would provide information relating to that day's work.

After booking on the driver took over responsibility for the locomotive. Testing of items such as injectors, gauge glasses, vacuum brake and sanding gear had to be carried out as soon as possible so that any defects could be corrected in plenty of time to avoid a late departure. Oiling around was an essential requirement which also gave the driver an opportunity to inspect the locomotive thoroughly. In essence the driver had to be satisfied that the locomotive allocated would perform the duties for which it was booked and that all equipment, including coal, water, sand and tools, met with requirements. It is not necessary to detail an inspection of a locomotive, the routine differed with type and space does not permit this as that inspection could be very detailed. What is important to understand is that the driver, and his fireman, had to check the machine completely in order that the driver might be satisfied as to its workable condition. Any defects had to be reported and if the driver was not satisfied as to the potential safety of his charge then the matter had to be brought to the attention of those in authority immediately.

Upon backing down and connecting to the train, brakes had to be tested in order to ensure that there was no leakage in the system and that they could be applied and released satisfactorily. This would be carried out in conjunction with the guard who had a vacuum gauge in his van. The guard would also inform the driver as to train load and any final instructions or changes with respect to the booked working. In past times when slip coach working was practised details of a slip had to be discussed with the relevant guard and arrangements agreed, the driver having to slow to a particular speed in order to achieve satisfactory slip. A check on train heating would also have to be made if a passenger train was being worked. If train load was such that two locomotives had to be used both footplate crews had to understand the road and any restrictions. Whistle signals between the locomotives ensured safe and correct operation of the train. Such signals were, of course, for a purpose and not to amuse the lineside enthusiast. An unwritten etiquette existed between footplate crews when double heading and one of the 'rules' concerned the taking of water at troughs. It was normal

practice for the train locomotive, the one connected to the carriages, to take water first with the lead or pilot loco picking up at some agreed point into the trough. If the lead locomotive took water first, its pick-up scoop action would disturb the water in the trough making it impossible for the following loco to pick up water at the same time. Should the lead loco be unable to lift its scoop in time the following machine might not collect any water. Brake application had similar agreements with the lead loco usually making the first application. As with other things different railways had slightly different ways of arranging matters but these general conditions applied.

In most cases single locomotive working applied and the notes which follow deal with normal operations. It should be understood, however, that different drivers have always had different ways of driving and there was never any set method which could be used for all cases. Even with the same class of locomotive drivers had slightly different ways of managing their charges and these could produce identical

Double heading, even in preservation, requires skill and understanding – Sir Lamiel *and 'Black Five'*
No 5407 at work near Armathwaite.

Duchess of Hamilton, *sanding gear in operation, starts a heavy train.*

results in terms of power and economy. It has already been mentioned in the section dealing with cylinders that some drivers would operate with full regulator and adjust by means of cut-off whilst others would vary both cut-off and regulator position, thus giving a variable steam chest pressure. Provided it did the job there was no effective difference, it was just driving technique.

When the guard's whistle indicated 'right away' the driver would check that the starting signal was 'off' and that the vacuum gauge read full vacuum showing that brakes were off. He would already have moved the reverser to its 'full gear' position and, after sounding his train whistle, would open the cylinder drain cocks and the regulator. Care had to be taken to avoid slipping and especially with a heavy train on a curve or in wet weather the sanding gear might be applied. The driver's skill would allow him to assess the situation and, almost without thinking, he would know what degree of cut-off to use and how far to open the regulator in order to put the train in motion without slipping. Should slipping occur it was necessary to shut off steam and restart more gently.

After a few turns of the wheels drain cocks were closed and as the train gathered speed adjustment in cut-off and regulator opening took place until the correct speed was reached. Obviously in some cases that meant a fully open regulator and adjustment of cut-off only. With the train on the move the driver could pay full attention to signals and speed restrictions. With most later locomotives devices for indicating speed were provided in the cab but many drivers would still assess speed by relation to exhaust beats and track noise. Such skills were not taught but came as a result of experience and a 'feel' for the locomotive and the railway environment. In good, or even moderate, visibility the driver could operate within his seeing distance but in fog he was very much on his own. Those intrinsic skills he had acquired over the years were beyond price. A difference in exhaust beat would tell him when gradients changed whilst sounds differed in cuttings and on embankments. With the introduction of advanced warning systems look-out problems were eased but vigilance was still essential.

Smells differed with location too, especially in an industrial area, but that sense of smell was used to advantage in assessing the condition of bearings. An experienced 'nose' could sense that something was wrong from the smell of overheating oil but some designers went further and provided capsules of strong smelling substances at certain bearings. At a particular temperature the capsule would release the substance giving the footplate crew a definite indication that a bearing was near to failing. The crew could then take action to slow down and seek a safe place in which to stop and inspect.

In the event of any failure which disabled the locomotive rapid action had to be taken to protect the train. Footplate crew needed to work in co-operation with the guard, informing the nearest signal box and placing detonators on the tracks to warn possible oncoming traffic. If the train had obstructed other running lines these also had to be protected.

Braking of a train required skill and judgement, it was not simply a case of applying the brake. That would certainly bring the train to rest but probably in the wrong place. A driver had to assess the braking capabilities of his train in relation to its size and running speed when the brakes were applied: if the stopping place was on a gradient, rising or falling, that too had to be taken into account.

Shutting off of steam at a particular point and gradual application of brakes could bring a train to rest at the desired location without any tugging effect. Stopping at a platform too early or too late could result in some coaches not being on the platform. If the train had to set back or make a double stop that caused delay.

A gentle stopping of the train resulted in less vacuum loss in the train pipe and so the large injector had less work to do in order to release the brakes. Brakes would normally have been released as soon as possible after the train came to rest with the tender hand brake then being used to keep the train in position: obviously the size of any gradient influenced these matters.

Different designers had driving positions on right- or left-hand sides of the cab and many drivers became accustomed to judging their stopping positions from markers on particular sides. If operating the same run with driving position shifted to the opposite side it could be difficult at first to assess the exact stopping position.

All drivers had their own ideas as to the best stance to adopt when driving and no hard and fast rules could ever be developed. Conditioning played an important part in attitude as did the amenities actually provided. GWR cabs with their hard tip-up seat were not exactly designed for comfort but they suited many footplate men of that company. Comforts provided by Bulleid on his 'Pacifics' and on the BR standard classes were not to the liking of everyone: it was simply a matter of conditioning. The important thing was that no matter what facilities were provided the footplate crew had to do its job efficiently and effectively. In most cases they did.

Preserved railways do not offer the length of run which was operated in steam days and the occasional main line steam excursion is not a true reflection of those days due to the many restrictions imposed. However, these are all that remain in Britain and the enthusiast, or merely interested, should be grateful that they are available to give an insight into work which was frequently long, hard and less glamorous than preservation, or the rose-tinted biographies, would have us believe.

APPENDIX

Nozzles

A nozzle may be defined as a duct of smoothly varying cross-sectional area. A fluid flowing through that duct will be subject to an energy transformation process. Depending upon the nature of the fluid, incompressible liquid such as water or compressible vapour such as steam, and the shape of the nozzle, convergent or divergent, pressure energy can be changed into velocity energy or vice versa.

As shown in the diagram there are two basic nozzle shapes, convergent and divergent, with a third, the convergent-divergent, being a combination of these. Exactly what happens in each case depends upon the fluid flowing and the pressure differences at each end of the nozzle. Analysis of the detailed situation involves some complex mathematics but this is unnecessary to understand what takes place.

Any fluid, water or steam, flowing through a convergent nozzle is subject to a pressure reduction and velocity increase thus the fluid is flowing much faster as it leaves the nozzle. How fast it flows depends upon the change in area and so the nozzles must be designed to suit particular conditions. The fireman's hose and garden hose are examples of convergent nozzles. A practical demonstration of the effect of reducing outlet area may be had from the experiment known to all schoolboys, a finger over the end of a bathroom or kitchen tap will produce an increasingly faster flowing jet of water as the outlet area is reduced. Such an experiment should only be carried out when

wife or mother is not in the vicinity and time is available to wipe up the resultant mess!

For a divergent nozzle the reverse effect may be obtained provided certain conditions apply. These need not be described but they involve speed of flow and type of fluid. With incompressible fluids such as water the divergent nozzle will cause a reduction in speed and an increase in pressure. With expansive fluids such as steam the reaction is different if the speed of flow is that of sound or above. A divergent

Different types of nozzles.

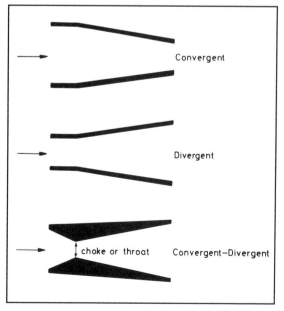

nozzle will then result in an even higher speed.

Usually the divergent nozzle is to be found in combination with a convergent form producing the convergent-divergent nozzle and the final result is the same as mentioned for the divergent nozzle. With a water flow the convergent section merely acts to combine the flow into a steady high speed stream and the divergent section acts to raise the pressure. Careful design of areas is needed to ensure a particular pressure is reached. With a compressive, and hence expansive, fluid such as steam the convergent part is used to increase velocity of the flow to sonic or supersonic speed and the divergent section then increases the speed even further. To suit particular conditions the taper on each part of the nozzle must be properly designed and it is essential that the diameter at the narrowest part, the choke or throat, is correct for the pressure change and amount of fluid flowing. An example of the convergent-divergent nozzle is to be found in the rocket engine where such an arrangement is used to produce a very high gas jet for propelling the rocket. As mentioned earlier nozzle design is a critical matter and each one really only suits a certain set of conditions: the basic points are that a convergent nozzle produces an increase in speed whilst a divergent nozzle results in higher pressure for water flow, but a higher speed for steam flow (provided the speed is already supersonic at the choke).

Index